Anne Stanesby is a solicitor who has worked in private practice, for a law centre and for the organisation Release. She is the author of the *Consumer Rights Handbook*, and has published widely in the field of legal advice. She lives in south London.

ANNE STANESBY

The
Criminal Justice
Handbook

A Guide for Women

First published by The Women's Press Ltd, 1999
A member of the Namara Group
34 Great Sutton Street, London EC1V 0LQ

Copyright © Anne Stanesby 1999

The right of Anne Stanesby to be identified as the author of this work
has been asserted by her in accordance with the Copyright, Designs
and Patents Act 1988.

British Library Cataloguing-in-Publication Data
A catalogue record for this book is available from the British Library.

ISBN 0 7043 4543 9

Typeset in Sabon 11/12pt by FSH Ltd, London
Printed and bound in Great Britain by Cox & Wyman Ltd,
Reading, Berkshire

Acknowledgements

I would like to thank Chris Tchiakovsky of Women in Prison, for her help with the chapter on prisons.

Contents

Introduction

Why write a handbook for women about our criminal justice system?

Most women will have some sort of encounter with the criminal justice system at least once during their lifetime. You may be asked to do jury service. You may witness a crime being committed and be asked to give evidence for the prosecution. You may unfortunately be the victim of a crime yourself. If so, you will probably be concerned that the offender be dealt with appropriately and you may also wish to claim compensation for any injuries. You might be accused of committing a crime yourself or you may be asked to give evidence on behalf of a friend who is in trouble.

Sometimes when a woman is caught up in any of the above situations she finds it a confusing and distressing experience. The reason for writing this book is to explain how the criminal justice system works in England and Wales and to offer practical guidance to women about how to deal with that system.

Why write such a book now?

Some types of legal advice are free at the moment. For instance, if you are under arrest in a police station a non-means-tested form of legal advice is available. But in most situations, legal aid is very strictly means-tested and only the very poorest people qualify. Legal aid has always been means-tested, but the test has in recent years become markedly more mean and undoubtedly the number of people who are eligible for legal aid assistance has declined. This would not matter too much if lawyers' fees were pitched at a level everyone could afford. But unfortunately most people find an hourly rate of, say, £125 per hour plus VAT too much to pay.

Other changes are in the pipeline as well. The government plans to allow only lawyers approved by them, to whom a government contract has been awarded, to do legal aid work in the future. This may well limit the number of lawyers that those who wish to use the legal aid system can choose between, which will be unfortunate, because if you need a lawyer then choosing a good one is of crucial importance.

What does all this add up to?

It means that now, particularly, women need to be well informed about our criminal justice system – how it works, how to assert themselves if caught up in it, and what sort of help is available to them from all sources, not just the legal profession.

What is the criminal law and how does it differ from civil law?

The authors Smith and Hogan, in their classic textbook on criminal law,[1] state that 'Crimes then are wrongs which judges have held, or parliament has from time to time laid down, are sufficiently injurious to the public to warrant the application of criminal procedures to deal with them.' It is the perceived injury to the public which makes the difference. If you are a house owner and you have a disagreement with your next-door neighbour about boundaries, then, if you cannot sort it out by agreement, the matter will have to be resolved in the civil courts. The dispute will be regarded as a purely private affair between you and your neighbour. But if your next-door neighbour breaks into your house and steals your possessions, then this would be regarded as sufficiently serious for the public to intervene. The police would arrest your neighbour for the offence of burglary and a government body, the Crown Prosecution Service (see Appendix II), would be responsible for dealing with any prosecution that later took place in the criminal courts. In the case of the boundary dispute, it would be up to you to take it to the civil court if you wanted your bit of land back.

What is a crime?

The ingredients of what constitutes a crime are, in the vast majority of cases, defined in a specific statute or Act of Parliament.[2] New statutes are being passed all the time. For example, the Protection from Harassment Act 1997 was passed to deal with the problem known as 'stalking'. Now it is a crime to 'pursue a course of conduct...which amounts to harassment of another'.[3] Some crimes, eg common assault and murder, are not defined in an actual statute, and lawyers rely on definitions laid down by judges or text-book writers. Occasionally, too, judges may effectively create new crimes by the way they decide a case.[4]

What sort of crimes are there?

Crimes can be crimes against the person. For example, homicidal crimes, which include the serious charge of murder, involving an element of intention to kill or to cause grievous bodily harm and carrying only one penalty, life imprisonment. Manslaughter is a less serious charge of homicide (and see further below). Assaults which do not result in death are divided into categories depending upon their seriousness: 'Assault occasioning actual bodily harm' is defined in a statute,[5] and is more serious than 'common assault'. Assaults resulting in grievous bodily harm are more serious still, particularly if the prosecution can prove that the accused intended such harm.[6] Rape is in a special category and is defined in the Sexual Offences Act 1956.

There are also property related crimes and these may involve an element of violence against the person as well. For instance, ordinary non-violent theft, such as shoplifting, is defined in the Theft Act 1968 in Section 1 (1). But if a person steals from another and is violent in the process, or puts the victim in fear of violence by, say, brandishing a knife at them, then the theft becomes the offence of robbery which is treated far more seriously.[7] The crime of burglary is also dealt with in the Theft Act[8] and is committed when a person enters a building as a trespasser and steals something inside it or inflicts grievous bodily harm on any person there.

Other types of crime include those relating to public order matters and the crime of criminal damage. There is even a Fraudulent Mediums Act of 1951.

Defences to crime

Sometimes conduct which would otherwise be criminal is not so because of circumstances. The person charged may have a defence to the charge against them. For example, a person who uses a reasonable degree of force in self-defence may not be guilty of murder or manslaughter if they kill their attacker. The Avon lady who let a man into her home thinking he wanted to buy after-shave, and who then stabbed him to death in self-defence when he attacked her with a flick knife and tried to rape her, was not prosecuted.[9]

Jacklyn Sheedy and Elizabeth Snook were accused of conspiracy to cause £605,000 of criminal damage to a crop of genetically modified maize. They were going to defend the case on the basis that they had a lawful excuse to damage the crops. Interestingly, in April 1999 a decision was made to drop the charges against them.

Reducing murder to manslaughter in cases involving women

Sometimes, too, a particular situation may make a crime less serious. Provocation or diminished responsibility may reduce what would be murder to manslaughter. After some considerable struggle, it has now been decided in a number of cases involving long standing patterns of violence against women by their partners that evidence of previous provocative acts or past conduct, particularly in cases of domestic violence, can be admitted in situations where murder is alleged.[10] In the case of Sara Thornton, her original conviction for murder was reduced after a retrial to one of manslaughter. Emma Thompson, who sadly died aged 30 on 11 July 1998 only 3 years after her release from prison, also eventually succeeded in having a conviction for murder reduced to manslaughter. She had been jailed for life at the age of 17 for the killing of a violent boyfriend.

There is also a special crime of infanticide defined in the Infanticide Act 1938. In cases where a woman is accused of killing her child of under 12 months, and at the time of the killing 'the balance of her mind was disturbed by reason of her not having fully recovered from the effect of giving birth to the child or by reason of the effect of lactation consequent upon the birth of the child', then the crime is to be treated as manslaughter not murder.

Children and people with mental disabilities

A person who is suspected of committing a crime may also be treated differently on account of their age or mental condition. A child under 10 cannot be prosecuted for a crime, although a new scheme is being introduced whereby criminal behaviour may result in a 'Child Safety Order' being made. If a person was mentally unwell at the time they committed an offence, this may provide them with a defence if intention is an essential ingredient of the offence; and if the offender suffered from diminished responsibility, this can reduce a crime of murder to one of manslaughter. This does not mean that mentally ill people get away with crimes. Even if they are too unwell to stand trial, a jury can still be empanelled to decide whether they were in fact guilty of the offence in question, and if a conviction follows the defendant will still be sentenced for any crime of which they have been found guilty.

How are women treated by the criminal justice system?

In the 12 months ending March 1998, a total of 4.5 million offences were recorded by the police in England and Wales. Ninety-one per cent of these crimes were property related and eight per cent were violent crimes.[11] The Home Office research document 'Aspects of Crime Gender 1996' states that for the period 1990–94 about a third of victims of violent crime were women and that 48 per cent of such crimes were perpetrated at the home of the victim or suspect as compared with only 18 per cent for men, which, as the document says, reflects 'the greater "domestic" nature of violence against women'.

In the 1990s there appears to have been a drop in the conviction rate for rape. In 1996, reported rapes rose to 5700, but less than a third resulted in prosecution, and only about 1 in 10 ended in a conviction.[12]

In the same year, 374 women per 100,000 of the population were found guilty of an offence or cautioned for an 'indictable' (serious) offence. The corresponding figure for men was 1839. Of the crimes committed by women, 83 per cent were for theft and handling stolen goods. The corresponding figure for men was 42 per cent. Of women found guilty of indictable offences, 10 per cent received immediate prison sentences, compared with 23 per cent of men. It was concluded by the Home Office that 'There are differences in the sentences men and women receive, but overall, women seem more likely to receive lenient sentences. This is so even when previous convictions are taken into account.'

One thing that no one can deny is that more women are being sent to prison than ever before. In 1992 there were 1577 women in prison; in 1999 the figure had increased to over 3000.

Not everyone in prison has committed a crime. Courts, including the civil courts, can send people to prison for 'contempt of court'. On 4 November 1997, pensioner Barbara Simpson was jailed for three months for ignoring an injunction obtained by her local council in a civil court. The injunction forbade her to put out food for birds on her giant 24-foot-square bird table.[13] Similarly, not everyone in prison has yet been found guilty of anything. Some people are remanded in custody pending their trial. In 1996, Angie Zeiter spent six months in Risley Remand Centre on remand for her alleged part in the disarming of a British Aerospace fighter-jet destined for Indonesia. She was ultimately found not guilty by a crown court jury.

Looking to the future

The reader should note that the Human Rights Act 1998, due to come into force on 2 October 2000, incorporates the provisions of the European Convention on Human Rights into our domestic law. This may have a dramatic effect on our criminal justice system. Article 3 says, for instance, 'No one shall be subjected to torture or to

inhuman or degrading treatment or punishment.' Article
5 deals with the liberty and security of the person and
Article 6 provides for the right to a fair hearing.

How this book is arranged

This book aims to give the reader practical advice about the
criminal justice system. Chapter 1 looks at the first
encounters you may have with the police and their
prosecuting body, the Crown Prosecution Service, and
advises about reporting a crime and obtaining protection in
that situation. It looks at your rights in your own home or
on the streets in the event of an encounter with the police,
and considers the pros and cons of staying silent when
questioned by the police. If you are taken to the police
station, it covers issues such as being stripped and searched
and your rights to things like phone calls and legal help.

Chapter 2 looks at the situation if you are appearing in
a criminal court for any reason. It considers who sits as
a judge or magistrate and what the rules are about juries.
It covers bail and the position of a person who has been
asked to give evidence, and gives advice about what to do
when fighting to maintain your innocence or when facing
an inevitable sentence.

Chapter 3 looks at women in prison, giving some pre-
sentence advice and discussing what may happen to you
in prison in respect of the disciplinary regime and your
rights to things like privileges and visits. It also considers
when and how you may be released.

In Chapter 4, some of the side effects of a brush with
the law are considered, including being fined or having
property confiscated. It also covers the effects on you and
your children, and the issues of publicity and having a
criminal record.

Chapter 5, the 'Fight Back' section, advises on making
a complaint, suing and prosecuting, obtaining compensation, representation at inquiries, and making appeals.

The section about obtaining advice and representing yourself is left to last. Chapter 6 gives advice about legal aid and lawyers, and about representing yourself if you have to or want to do this. Lastly, it covers the issue of being an 'appropriate adult' to someone who is under 17 or has a mental disability and is under arrest in a police station.

Appendix I details various advice agencies or pressure groups that you might find helpful to approach with your particular problem. Appendix II lists and explains the function of various official bodies. A list of recommended reading is included as Appendix III.

Unfortunately, it is not possible in a book of this length to give specific advice about each type of criminal offence in which the reader may become involved. Nor is it possible to outline comprehensively how the youth justice criminal justice system works or how our criminal justice system deals with those who have a mental disability (although I do include some details about both). Hopefully the contents of Chapter 6 and the Appendices will point you in the right direction, whatever problem you have with the criminal justice system.

Chapter 1
First Encounters, the Police and the Crown Prosecution Service

This chapter deals with the initial stages of a woman's involvement with the criminal justice system. If you are a victim of a crime you must, as soon as you can, consider reporting that crime to the correct authorities, and you may well wish to seek protection once you have done so. This aspect is dealt with in the first section, 'Reporting a Crime and Obtaining Protection'. In the next section, 'Homes and Streets', I detail your rights if the police wish to gain entry to your home or if they wish to stop and search you on the street. In 'Silence Isn't Golden', I explain what the law says about your obligation to answer any questions put to you by the police and what inferences can be drawn if you remain silent. 'At the Station' describes how to obtain legal advice if you are detained. 'Strips and Searches' and 'Taking Samples' detail the legal provisions governing police officers' rights to perform these procedures, as many women find such experiences very distressing. Lastly, 'Other Rights in the Police Station', details how long you can be detained and other information, such as your rights to make phone calls.

Reporting a Crime and Obtaining Protection

Even though we know that crime goes on all the time, it is still a great shock to be the victim of crime. It can be difficult to think straight, but it's important to know what your options are, so you can decide how best to proceed.

The Victim's Charter

The Victim's Charter, published by the Home Office Commission Directorate,[1] is supposedly a 'statement of service standards for victims of crime'. It does not have the force of law, but if its principles are not adhered to the unsatisfied victim would have a good basis to complain and also to insist their requirements be dealt with. There might also be other pursuable remedies (see Chapter 5).

Report the crime as soon as possible

However awful you feel, it is probably in your best interests to report a crime as soon as possible. Obviously there is more chance that the perpetrator will be caught if you report the event as soon as it occurs, but also any failure to report a crime promptly, without good reason, could be used against you if you later wish to claim compensation. The Criminal Injuries Compensation Agency (see Appendix II) gives a specific warning about this, which I give more details about in Chapter 5.[2]

Is it worth it?

The reasons for not reporting a crime can range from apathy – for example, feeling it's too much trouble 'because it's not covered by insurance' in the case of property loss – to pure terror – of those, for example, who know that reporting the crime will inevitably lead to victimisation. Some people also feel that the police are simply not interested when they are the victim of a crime. Members of ethnic minority groups, for instance, may feel that the police are not interested in protecting them from racial harassment. The Crime and Disorder Act 1998 does now make special provision for 'racially aggravated offences', so that when an offence occurs, if it can be shown that the offender demonstrated towards the victim hostility based on the victim's membership (or presumed membership) of a racial group, then a more serious penalty can be imposed.[3] So it may be worth it after all, and if you need protection you should get it.

No one knows how many crimes are unreported and therefore unrecorded, but it is acknowledged by the Home Office that 'A large proportion of crime is unrecorded, as many offences are not reported to the police.'[4] Don't make the crime against you swell these numbers.

Taking the plunge

If you do decide to go to the police station, and you are nervous or frightened, then take a friend with you. If no one is available you could try telephoning the organisation Victim Support (see Appendix I), as one of their volunteers should be able to accompany you.

- The Victim's Charter states that if you phone the police to tell them about a crime they will send an officer to see you if necessary. If you are disabled or injured, unwell or frightened to go out and you would rather not go to the police station then quote this to them.
- If you have been raped or sexually abused then you will probably be asked to undergo a medical examination. You have the right to be treated in a sensitive fashion and there are a number of specialist advice agencies you could consult, see Appendix I; you may also wish to read *Sexual Violence* by the London Rape Crisis Centre, also published by The Women's Press (see Appendix III).

- The police will also want to take a statement from you and if you need an interpreter the police can and should arrange this.

Tell the police if you are afraid of further episodes

The Victim's Charter says the police should ask you about fears of further victimisation. It is important to emphasise very clearly if you have reason to fear further similar episodes. This is important because if the offender is later caught and charged they do not have to be released on bail and if they are there are all sorts of conditions that can be imposed such as where they must live, places where they may not go and, most importantly, a condition that they do not contact you. Breach of these conditions could and should, where appropriate, result in bail being refused in the future.

Tell the police how the crime has affected you

The Victim's Charter states that you can expect 'the chance to explain how the crime has affected you, and your interests to be taken into account'. The police are supposed to ask you about details of your loss, damage or injury. This is important because, as you will see in Chapter 5, the criminal court can order the offender to pay you compensation – a much easier way of obtaining it than having to sue in the civil court. The police will also give a report to the Criminal Injuries Compensation Agency if you later claim compensation from them.

The Charter says in addition that the police, Crown Prosecution Service, magistrates and judges will take the information you give at the police station into account when making their decisions. In other words, what you say about how the crime has affected you can in turn affect the decision as to whether the offender is charged, whether they are released on bail and what sort of sentence they get if found guilty. It is very important therefore to give the police all the relevant details.

Keeping you informed

- The Victim's Charter says that the police will do their best to catch the person responsible for your crime and will keep you informed of significant developments in your case – for example, whether someone has been caught, cautioned or charged. (The proposed Freedom of Information Bill may give you more rights in the future in this respect.)
- The Victim's Charter also says that if the accused person is released on bail, the police will do their best to tell you as quickly as possible. They should also tell you if there are any conditions attached to the bail and advise you what to do if those conditions are broken.
- The Statement of National Standards of Witness Care in the Criminal Justice System (July 1996)[5] also states, in paragraph 18.1, 'The court should inform the police immediately if bail is granted to any defendant who was in custody, and supply the police with details of any bail conditions. As a matter of urgency, and in any event within 24 hours of receiving the information from the court, the police should notify those witnesses who have previously expressed concern about the defendant being granted bail or conditional bail.'
- You should also be asked if you wish to receive further information about the progress of your case. Always say yes.

The Crown Prosecution Service

If you do ask to be kept informed, you will be told about any decision to drop or alter the charges 'substantially'. This is where the Crown Prosecution Service comes in. If the police do decide to charge someone with an offence against you, it is the CPS who decide whether to go on with the prosecution. There is a Code of Practice for Crown Prosecutors which sets out the basic principles which they should follow when they make case decisions. The June 1994 Code for Crown Prosecutors states that there are two stages in the decision to prosecute. The first stage is the evidential test. The Crown Prosecutors must be satisfied that there is enough evidence to provide a 'realistic prospect of conviction' against each defendant on each charge. The second stage is the public interest test. Factors which are considered are the seriousness of the offence and the circumstances of the offender. The Code gives examples of what sort of things would be considered to be serious in this context. For example, 'the victim of the offence was vulnerable, has been put in considerable fear, or suffered personal attack, damage or disturbance ... a weapon was used or violence was threatened during the commission of the offence.' The Code also gives examples of the sort of considerations which might lead to the CPS not prosecuting on the public interest ground – if, for instance, 'the defendant is elderly or is, or was at the time of the offence, suffering from significant mental or physical ill health' – although these in turn may be disregarded if 'the offence is serious or there is a real possibility that it may be repeated'.

The CPS has come in for a lot of criticism recently. There has been a lot of controversy, for example, about some CPS decisions not to prosecute in certain cases, such as their seeming reluctance to prosecute men who are charged with sexual assaults upon women with learning difficulties. The organisation Voice was set up mainly to protest and campaign about this (see Appendix I). There has also been concern about failures to prosecute police officers following deaths after arrest and in custody. A major review of the service, the Glidewell Inquiry, reported in June 1998 and the CPS has now been reorganised. It is hoped, therefore, that things will improve. If you are not satisfied with a CPS decision in relation to your case then see what to do in Chapter 5. You can also see there what to do if the police or the courts do not deal with your case as you feel they should have done.

Future protection

Even if the person who attacked or harassed you is arrested and sent to prison you may still continue to be afraid of them. The Victim's Charter says that if s/he is sentenced to life imprisonment or if s/he has committed a serious sexual or violent crime, then you can expect the probation service, who should contact you within two months of the sentence to discuss your wishes in this respect, to let you know when s/he is likely to be released. In the case of sex offenders, the Crime and Disorder Act 1998 provides that the police may apply to their local magistrates' court to obtain an order imposing prohibitions on the person's behaviour after their release.[6]

Homes and Streets

Even if you have not been the victim of a crime, just about everyone is likely to have some sort of encounter with the police at some time. You might be walking down the street or driving or cycling on the road, or you might be in your own home, when suddenly the police want to ask you questions or conduct a search.

There is no doubt that those in positions of authority consider that every citizen has a moral and social duty to be helpful to the police.[7] It is up to you to make up your mind about this; there is no legally enforceable duty imposed upon you. However, people in authority, and sometimes ordinary citizens, do have rights to impinge upon your freedoms in certain circumstances. These rights are provided mainly by statutes or Acts of Parliament. The

Police and Criminal Evidence Act 1984 (PACE) is the major Act in this area but there are lots of other statutes which are also relevant. Under the provisions of PACE, the government of the day must issue Codes of Practice setting out the details of how these powers ought to be exercised. Code A deals with police powers to 'stop and search' members of the public who are out and about. Code B deals with the searching of premises by police officers.

Unless you have an encyclopedic memory, the chances of your being able to recall exactly what your legal rights are when confronted by a police officer are about nil. However, there are some basic details which are worth trying to remember.[8] Firstly, there are certain types of activity, eg driving a car, which of themselves give those in authority the right to interfere with your progress. I deal with these situations first. Secondly, I deal with rights to interfere with you just because you happen to be out in a public place.[9] Lastly, I set out what to do if you are in your own home and the police want to come in.

As a general rule it is probably most sensible to be polite to the police, however much you want them to go away and leave you alone. If you start a dispute with them you might find yourself being arrested for breach of the peace or obstruction. Try to keep calm, even if you are panicking. **On the other hand, if a person who is not in uniform tries to stop you or to get into your house, always demand to see their identification. If the person is a police officer you are entitled to make this request and if the person does not comply you should immediately assume that they are bogus and try and get away from them or shut the door in their face.**

Out and about

There are certain situations when the police do have specific rights to stop you when you may be on your way somewhere.

Driving a car

If a police officer in uniform asks you to stop, you must do so. If asked, you must provide your name and address and if asked you must produce your driving documents on the spot or at a police station on a later date.[10]

Cycling

Again, if a police officer in uniform requires you to stop, you must do so. If it is alleged that you have been guilty of dangerous, careless or inconsiderate cycling then, if asked, you must give your name and address.[11]

Walking

If a police officer has been directing the traffic and you have ignored their directions then, if they ask you, you must give your name and address.[12]

Being stopped and searched in a public place

In certain circumstances the police are also entitled to stop and search you and your vehicle. In most cases the police must have 'reasonable grounds' for suspecting that they will find such items as stolen goods, prohibited drugs or offensive weapons. So far as the latter are concerned, however, recent legislation allows the police to stop and search you sometimes just because you happen to be in a particular area at a particular time.[13]

Before any search takes place the police officer must tell you his or her name, the name of their police station, the object of the search and the grounds for undertaking it. An officer not in uniform must show you their warrant card.[14] The police officer is not allowed to make you remove any of your clothing in public other than an outer coat, jacket or gloves. The police officer must (unless there is a very good reason why not) make a record of what happens at this search and you are entitled to be provided with a copy of this record as long as you ask for it within the next 12 months.

Concern has been expressed about the disproportionate number of black people who have been stopped and searched by police under the purported exercise of these powers.[15] The police are not supposed to stop someone just because they are black: 'A person's colour, age, hairstyle or manner of dress...cannot be used alone or in combination with each other as the sole basis on which to search that person. Nor may it be founded on the basis of stereotyped images of certain persons or groups as more likely to be committing offences.'[16]

Being arrested on the street

In certain circumstances the police are entitled to arrest you on the street, even though no warrant has been issued for your arrest. Under PACE, they can do this if you have committed, are in the act of committing, or are suspected on 'reasonable grounds' of having committed, an 'arrestable offence'. It's impossible to list here all the offences included in this definition[17] but any offence for which anyone over 21 could be sentenced in the crown court to five years' imprisonment and upwards is included.

The police can also arrest you if they have 'reasonable grounds' for suspecting that you have committed another less serious offence if certain criteria apply.[18] You can also be arrested for breach of the peace.

It is worth noting that an arrest is not lawful if you are not informed that you have been arrested and why.[19]

At home

If a uniformed police officer or a person who has produced police id calls at your house they may just be seeking your assistance – for example, if someone has just been attacked in the street outside your house – or they may want to come in to your house for some reason, for example, to arrest someone.[20]

They may also want to conduct a search for certain items. In theory you do not have to agree to let them in unless a search warrant has been issued by your local magistrates or if other specified criteria apply. For instance, the police are allowed to come in without a warrant to deal with or prevent a breach of the peace. But don't forget that, in any event, you are entitled to be told why they wish to come in.

If you do consent to a search, then, for it to be lawful, you should be asked to sign a notice to that effect. A notice should be given to you even if you did not consent to the entry, and one should be left for you if you were not there at the time. This notice should set out the basis upon which the search is being conducted and should specify your rights, eg to compensation for any damage caused and in relation to seized property. If a warrant has been issued you should be given a copy of it.

If you wish, you can ask a friend, neighbour or other person to witness the search. The police must agree to this unless there are reasonable grounds for believing 'that this would seriously hinder the investigation or endanger the officers concerned or other people'.[21] Having someone else with you will help you through this, so take advantage of this right.

As may be apparent from the above, the practical reality is that if the police feel like stopping you on the street or coming into your home there is not much you can do about it at the time, however unjustified you think their behaviour is. But if the police have behaved oppressively or unlawfully then you may be able to sue them for damages or at least to make a complaint about what has happened, see Chapter 5. Never feel that you have to accept any violation of your rights.

Silence Isn't Golden

Wherever any encounter between you and the police takes place, be it on the street, in your home or in the police station, the time may come when the police are asking you questions and you are wondering whether you should answer them or remain silent. At one time this was a relatively easy situation to deal with, as anyone suspected of or accused of committing a crime had the right to remain silent and no one could hold that against them. But the Criminal Justice and Public Order Act 1994 changed all that. Now, in certain carefully prescribed circumstances, if you remain silent in the face of police questioning it could later be held against you.

The rules work like this:

- If you are arrested by a police officer and there is any suspicious object, substance or mark on you or in your possession, and if the officer tells you they consider this item to be suspicious and asks you to make an explanation and you refuse to do so, then the court that tries you later 'may draw such inferences from the failure or refusal as appear proper'. The officer must warn you in 'ordinary language' what the effect of your failure to answer these questions would be.[22]
- If you are arrested by a police officer and have been found by them at a place, at or about the time the offence for which you have been arrested is supposed to have been committed, and the officer reasonably believes that your presence in that place at that time may be because you took part in the offence, and you are told this by the officer and you

fail to account for your presence at this location, then the same result can occur. Once again, you must be warned in ordinary language of the likely result of a failure to answer.[23]

- If, even before you are charged,[24] you hear the words of the caution – **'You do not have to say anything. But it may harm your defence if you do not mention when questioned something which you later rely on in court. Anything you do say may be given in evidence'** – you must go on red alert. If you are then questioned by a constable 'trying to discover whether or by whom the offence had been committed' and you then fail 'to mention any fact relied on in [your] defence', then once again the court which tries you may draw 'such inferences from the failure as appear proper'. The fact you failed to mention must be one 'which in the circumstances existing at the time the accused could reasonably have been expected to mention'.[25]

- If you are charged with an offence or are officially informed that you might be prosecuted for it and you fail to mention the same type of facts as above, in the same type of circumstances, then the same result can occur.[26]

All of this could put you in a difficult position. If, for instance, the police telephone you at home and ask you to come to the police station to answer some questions, then obviously you have got the chance to get hold of a lawyer to help you. If things blow up in the street or if your case comes into the category where the police are allowed to exclude your lawyer, then you may have to deal with the situation on your own. It is therefore very important that you yourself are aware of the implications of your situation.

In certain circumstances, as I have set out above, if you

do not answer questions, reasonably put, about a suspected offence, and you are charged with that offence and tried for it, your silence could be held against you at the trial. This can apply even if you remained silent because your lawyer advised you to. You could not be found guilty just on the basis of suspiciously remaining silent alone, but, if there is other evidence, then remaining silent at this point could be very incriminating. However, if there is no other evidence, then admitting it could put you into a frame where you would not have been otherwise.

Other points to note: if you later plead guilty and it can be said that you were helpful to the police and readily admitted your guilt, that will be a point in your favour when it comes to sentencing. Also the police don't always have to charge you with the offence. They could, if the offence is considered to be not very serious – eg, possession of a small amount of cannabis – decide to caution you instead.[27] This means you won't have to go to court and be sentenced and you will not get a criminal conviction with all the disadvantages that brings. However, you can't even be considered for a caution unless you admit the offence. This does not mean that you should say you are guilty when you are not, just because you would rather be cautioned than fight it out in court. Unfortunately, even being cautioned could have some effects on you later. See Chapter 4, and do always get legal advice before agreeing to a caution.

At the Station

How to get legal help if you are detained in a police station

If you are detained in a police station then you have certain rights to obtain legal advice. You may consult and communicate with a solicitor privately at any time, whether in person, in writing or by telephone. The police must tell you about this right and the fact that independent legal advice is available free of charge from the duty solicitor.[28] The fact that you were or were not told of this right ought to be recorded on a document called a custody record on which certain details regarding your sojourn in the police station will be recorded. The police will also note down whether you did or did not ask for a lawyer or if you refused to give any answer. Note that if you say you want legal advice the police should not usually interview you until you get it.[29]

The person who does the recording is called the custody officer/sergeant. This officer must not be involved in the investigation into whatever crime you are accused of. The contents of the custody record can be of crucial importance later on if you are put on trial or if you wish to sue the police for, say, false arrest. You and your lawyers will be able to get hold of a copy provided you ask for it within 12 months, and any lawyer coming to see you in the police station will be allowed to look at it.[30]

There are some circumstances, however, in which the police are allowed to stop you consulting a lawyer and may proceed to interview you without you having legal help. If you are being held on suspicion of having committed a 'serious arrestable offence', then the police are allowed, if certain criteria apply, to delay your rights to access to a lawyer for up to 36 hours maximum (48 hours for suspected terrorists).[31]

In many cases the interview ought to be tape recorded,[32] but if an old style note-taking interview takes place make sure you are taking notes too and when asked to sign, as you should be, make sure that the record made by the police is accurate. Check it very carefully and don't be afraid to insist that necessary amendments be made. Paragraph 11 of Code of Practice C deals with interviews and says that the interviewing officer must not try to obtain answers to questions or elicit a statement by the use of oppression.

If the person being interviewed appears to be under 17 or has a mental disability then an 'appropriate adult' must be called in. See the section about this in Chapter 6.

Strips and Searches

One of the worst things about being arrested and taken into custody is the fear of humiliation and invasion of body space. The rules about what the police are allowed to do in respect of searching you, taking body samples from you and photographing and fingerprinting you are contained mostly in PACE and the Codes of Practice. People often go to a police station voluntarily to answer questions or to make enquiries. It is important to understand that it is only once you have been arrested that you can be subjected to search-type procedures.

If you are arrested at a police station or arrive at one already under arrest, you can be subjected to the following procedures.

The basic search

The custody officer is under a duty to ascertain what property you have on you and for that purpose they may search you to 'the extent that s/he consider necessary'. You must be searched by a constable of the same sex. Only outer clothing may be removed. Clothing and personal effects can only be taken from you if certain criteria apply and, except in certain situations, you must be given the reason for them being taken.[33]

The strip-search

Sometimes it is lawful to strip-search you. This is only allowed if the police have reasonable grounds to believe that you are hiding an article which you would not be allowed to keep.[34] A note must be made on your custody record as to why it was considered necessary to put you through this. A strip-search 'shall not be routinely carried out where there is no reason to consider that articles have been concealed'. You must not be strip-searched in an area where you can be seen by persons 'who do not need to be present' and anyone of the opposite sex. In most cases, if exposure of intimate parts of the body will take place, then at least two people must be present.[35]

A strip-search must be conducted with 'proper regard to the sensitivity and vulnerability of the person in these circumstances and every reasonable effort shall be made to secure the person's co-operation and minimise embarrassment'. The search should be conducted as quickly as possible and you should be allowed to get dressed again as soon as it is all over. People who are searched should not normally be required to have all their clothes removed at the same time, 'for example, a woman shall be allowed to put on her blouse and upper garments before further clothing is removed'. When necessary to assist the search, the person may be required to hold her arms in the air or to stand with her legs apart and to bend forward so that a visual examination only may be made of the genital and anal areas.

The intimate search

Sometimes an 'intimate search' may be carried out. This is a search 'which consists of the physical examination of a person's body orifices other than the mouth'.[36] Such searches are only allowed if the police have grounds for believing that you are concealing a certain type of item which can only be found if such a search is conducted. These items are things which you might use to harm yourself or others, and Class A drugs.[37] Usually, a doctor or nurse must carry out an intimate search,[38] but they do not have to be of the same sex as you. Drugs searches have to take place at hospitals, surgeries or other medical premises. The same rules about privacy, etc, apply as set out above. A record of which parts of your body were searched and why must be made.

Taking Samples

As well as being searched, other types of procedures can be carried out.

Intimate samples

Sometimes 'intimate samples' can be taken from you. These are:

- a sample of blood, semen or any other tissue fluid, urine or pubic hair
- a dental impression
- a swab taken from a person's body orifice other than the mouth.[39]

A senior police officer must authorise this procedure on the basis that there are reasonable grounds for suspecting your involvement in a recordable offence[40] and for believing that the taking of the sample will tend to confirm or disprove your involvement. However, you do also have to consent.[41] If you do not consent then an adverse inference can be drawn from that refusal at your trial. You must be warned about this and if you hear such a warning then do take legal advice about what to do. The samples, except for urine, must be taken by doctors or dentists.

Non-intimate samples

Non-intimate samples can be taken even if you do not consent (and you will always be asked to consent first) if an authorisation is given in the same circumstances as above.[42] The reason must be recorded. A non-intimate sample includes a sample of hair other than pubic hair. These may be taken by cutting the hair or by plucking hairs with their roots so long as no more are plucked than the person taking the sample 'reasonably considers to be necessary for a sufficient sample'(!) Other non-intimate samples include nail scrapings, swabs from the external parts of the body and the mouth, footprints and other body prints (except fingerprints).

Fingerprints

Again, fingerprints can be taken if you do not consent, if an authorisation is given on the same basis as above. Again, you must be told the reason and it must be recorded. You may also be fingerprinted after you have been charged with or reported for a recordable offence or after conviction.[43]

Photographs

Photographs may be taken if you consent or if it is considered necessary for certain identification purposes.[44]

In most cases all samples, fingerprints and photographs must be destroyed if you are later found not guilty or if a decision is made not to prosecute or caution you.[45] The destruction must take place as soon as practicable after the conclusion of the proceedings or after the decision is taken not to proceed. Copies of the prints must also be destroyed and access to computer data relating to them must be made impossible. You may insist on witnessing the destruction and you may demand a certificate regarding the computer data.

Other Rights in the Police Station

It is important to remember that if you are in a police station and have not been arrested then you are legally free to go. If you are brought to the police station under arrest or are arrested whilst you are there, then you are not legally free to go. This does not mean that you have no rights whatsoever. You have rights which are set out in the Police and Criminal Evidence Act and the Codes of Practice.

How long can they keep you for?

The position is different depending upon whether or not you have been charged. Once you are charged with something then, unless certain criteria apply, you should be released. However, the police may impose conditions on this release in certain circumstances.[46]

Adults[47] who have been charged can only be kept on in the police station in the following circumstances:

- if their name and address cannot be established
- if it is suspected that false details have been provided
- if there are grounds to believe they would abscond, or interfere with the investigation
- if detention is necessary for their own protection
- if the offence is 'imprisonable' and they might commit another offence
- if it is not imprisonable but they might injure someone or damage property.[48]

The good news is that, if detained after charge, you must be taken to the next sitting of the local magistrates' court where you can ask for bail.[49]

If you are not yet charged then you are still entitled to be released, albeit on conditions,[50] but the police may keep you in if this is necessary to secure or preserve evidence relating to an offence for which you are under arrest, or to obtain such evidence by questioning you.

You must be told why you are being detained and a record of the reason should be made.[51] To start with you can only be held for 24 hours. This can be increased to up to 36 hours if, in addition to the above reason, you are under arrest for a serious arrestable offence.[52] The investigation must be being conducted in a 'diligent and expeditious' fashion. Further detention can only be authorised by the local magistrates' court, and they can only extend it to a maximum of 96 hours (dating from when you were first taken into custody).[53]

What can you do about all this? Whether or not you have been charged your detention has to be reviewed periodically. Subject to certain permissible delays, reviews must take place firstly after six hours and thereafter every nine hours. You or your solicitor, or, at the discretion of the review officer,[54] anyone with an interest in your welfare, may make representations about the continued detention.[55] If an application is made to the magistrates you are entitled to legal representation. If you have children or other dependants that is a powerful argument for you to be released as soon as possible.

Keeping in touch with the outside world

If you are arrested and taken to a police station your first thought may well be to make sure that someone outside knows what has happened to you. This would obviously be the case, for instance, if you had left your children with a babysitter. A detained person is entitled, if they ask, to tell one friend, relative or other person who is known to them or who is likely to take an interest in their welfare, as soon as is practicable and at public expense, that they have been arrested and where they are being held.[56] But if you are being held on suspicion of having committed a 'serious arrestable offence' and certain criteria apply,[57] then the police are allowed to delay giving you this right, but only for up to a maximum of 36 hours (unless you are suspected of terrorism, when this period increases to 48 hours). You are warned that, unless you are telephoning your solicitor, anything you say on the telephone may be 'listened to as appropriate and may be given in evidence'.[58]

If the worst happens and no one answers or you get an answer machine, what then? If you cannot contact the person you want to get hold of, you can choose up to two alternative people to try. If they too are unavailable the police have a discretion to allow further attempts until you have been able to tell someone where you are.[59] You also have the right to be supplied with writing materials on request and you may also speak on the telephone for a reasonable time to one person.[60] The police have a discretion to pay for these communications. You may also receive visits at the custody officer's discretion and he or she should allow the visits where possible.[61] Finally, if an enquiry as to your whereabouts is made by a friend, relative or person with an interest in your welfare, they must be told what has happened to you, provided you agree, unless your offence is in the 'serious' category when the same criteria apply.[62]

There are other provisions in Code of Practice C about what your conditions of detention ought to be like and about matters such as medical treatment. There is not space to list them all here, but Paragraph 1.2 of Code C does say 'This Code of Practice must be readily available at all police stations for consultation by police officers, detained persons and members of the public.'

In the 'Silence Isn't Golden' section I mentioned the rights you have to access to legal advice. If you are worried about your children, then the solicitor should be able to assist you by making representations that you should be released and by making telephone calls to whoever is caring for your children to check everything is all right. If new arrangements have to be made for your children which involve social services, for example, the solicitor should be able to advise you about this. Don't panic. As long as you can show you have acted responsibly at all times this will be a strong point in your favour when it comes to getting the children back.

If an independent police station visitor[63] happens to turn up while you are being detained you should be asked if you want to speak to them. Take advantage of this if you are unhappy about anything, including the state of the place or the food but particularly if you haven't had your phone call or have been denied access to a solicitor.

Chapter 2
In the Criminal Courts

In this chapter I explain how the criminal courts work, both from the point of view of a victim or of a witness to a crime and of a person who is themselves on trial. Less serious criminal offences are tried in magistrates' courts, although even those charged with more serious offences will make their first appearance in these courts. More serious offences such as rape or murder are tried in the crown court and it is there that you find judges sitting with juries in cases where the defendant is pleading 'not guilty'. Some offences can be tried in either court and at present, in relation to those types of offences, the defendant may choose which one to be tried in. (Civil cases are dealt with in the county court, although higher value or more serious cases are tried in the appropriate section of the High Court.) There are rights to appeal to higher courts.[1]

In the first section of this chapter I explain what sort of person sits as a magistrate or judge, and the rules about juries. In the next section I consider the issue of bail, ie release into the community while awaiting a trial, which is an important issue both for victims and for defendants. In the third section I look at your rights if you have been asked to give evidence. In the fourth I explain what to expect if you are pleading 'not guilty'. In the fifth I deal with the issue of sentencing in cases where the defendant has pleaded, or has been found, guilty.

Magistrates, Judges and Juries

When it comes to sentencing, gender doesn't come into it. We follow the judicial oath which promises to be fair to all men.

Magistrates Association response to allegations that women are more likely than men to be jailed for minor offences.[2]

The fact that a judge might have fallen asleep during a criminal trial did not necessarily mean that prejudice had been caused to the defendant and any allegation of such a kind had to be specific and made at the time so that it could be known which parts of the evidence the judge was supposed to have missed.[3]

If you have been asked to appear as a witness for the prosecution or defence or if you have been accused of a crime then you need to know something about the person who will be judging the issues.

Magistrates

When a person has been accused of a crime, however serious, they must appear first in the magistrates' court upon whose patch the crime was committed. There are two sorts of magistrates who sit in these courts. Neither wear any special robes and both sit on a raised platform behind a table at the back of the court.

If there is only one magistrate sitting there then you know this person is a 'stipendiary magistrate'. This means that they are doing this as their full time job and are getting paid a generous salary for doing so. These magistrates have to have legal qualifications and a minimum of seven years' practising experience. They sit mostly in large cities. An important point to note is that a stipendiary magistrate is a professional lawyer sitting day after day in the magistrates' court, and very little will come up which she or he has not heard a million times before.

If you see more than one magistrate then you are appearing before the lay justices. These people have no legal qualifications and are not receiving a salary for carrying out this function. A person who does not have a criminal record is eligible to apply to perform this function.

There are no juries in the magistrates' courts. If you are tried in a magistrates' court it is the magistrates who will decide whether you are guilty or not guilty and, if you are sentenced there, what sentence to give you.

A point to note about magistrates is that they will always strive to follow the letter of the law, however much they might personally disagree with that law. Therefore, if you are guilty of the offence according to the law but wish to invite the court to acquit you on the grounds that the law is immoral or that you were justified on moral grounds for breaking it, then the magistrates' court is not the venue for you. If you have the right to demand jury trial in this situation you must take it if you want to get anywhere with these types of arguments.

Judges

If the case is in the crown court then we start to find formal legal dress. The judge will be wearing a wig and a collection of robes, the style of which will depend on how senior a judge he or she is. If the case is very serious, he or she will be a High Court Judge. In other cases they will be a more junior judge called a circuit judge, or they may be a lawyer who is being tried out called a 'recorder'. They must be an experienced lawyer and are paid a lot of money. Judicial posts at this level do now have to be advertised, the Lord Chancellor having recently said that all eligible people who apply will be considered. However, the Lord Chancellor still has to recommend the person and the age-old system of taking 'secret soundings' no doubt still flourishes and is blamed by some for the large number of white men who sit on the Bench.[4] Applicants will be expected to declare if they are freemasons and all those appointed before this rule came in have since been asked this question.[5]

Judges cannot decide whether you are guilty or not guilty. That is the function of the jury, although the judge plays a very important part in helping them reach their decision because the judge will advise the jury about the law and will sum up the evidence to the jury at the very end of the case. The judge is also the one who decides what sentence an accused person should get if the jury finds them guilty (or if they plead guilty in the first place).

If you object to the decision made by a judge or a magistrate then you may have a right of appeal. You can also complain about the personal conduct of judges or magistrates – see Chapter 5, 'Fight Back'.

Juries

At present, those accused of a wide range of offences have an absolute right to request jury trial, although the government plans to restrict this right.[6] Jurors are chosen in the first instance at random from the electoral roll. If you are selected you will receive a form called a jury summons. This explains who is excluded from jury service and who is entitled to be excused. This is important; the fact that you have been sent the summons does not automatically mean that you should or must serve.

- Jurors must be at least 18 and under 70.
- People with certain types of criminal convictions and mental disabilities are excluded from being able to sit as jurors, as are those who work in court-related situations, eg lawyers, police officers and the clergy.
- Certain people have the right to be excused, ie politicians, medical personnel and members of the armed services.
- You can also ask to be excused from serving if you are over 65, or if you have been on jury service during the past 2 years, or if you served before on a particularly long or awful trial and were excused for a period which has not yet expired. Other people can ask to be excused if they have a special problem and you can ask for your jury service to be deferred to another date.

Being asked to do jury service can be pretty tedious – there can be a lot of waiting around. It can also be very distressing – for instance, if you are asked to serve on a rape trial. Unfortunately no one has thought to give any support to traumatised jurors and the jury members are left to support each other when highly stressed.

Remember that it is the judge's job to explain all necessary legal points to the jury, such as the fact that you should not find the person guilty unless you are sure beyond reasonable doubt that the person is guilty. If there is any legal point that puzzles you then make sure that a note setting out your concerns is passed to the judge so that they can explain the matter.

Jurors can claim for loss of earnings, travelling expenses and a meal allowance, and when you receive your jury summons you should also be sent the booklet 'You and Your Jury Service' which details your rights in this respect.

The jurors will be asked to take an oath promising to discharge their duty properly. Before they do this the accused person must be told of their right to challenge (ie object to) the jurors who have been selected. Although it is possible for the accused person to challenge the entire jury this is very rare. An accused person may challenge individual jurors after the juror's name has been called and before the juror has been sworn, but the accused person must give a reason for this challenge. The sort of reasons which are relevant are, for instance, if the accused knows the juror is disqualified from serving, if it can be alleged that the juror has some personal defect which makes them incapable of discharging their duties as a juror, or that they are not impartial.

The Courts' Charter contains a leaflet setting out what jurors are entitled to expect from the court service, so see Chapter 5, 'Fight Back', for advice about complaining if you feel you have been badly treated.

Bail

If the police refuse to release an accused person from the police station then, as we have seen, the person must appear at the magistrates' court as soon as possible. There the magistrates must decide whether the person should now be released and if so whether that release should or should not be on conditions. Whether you have been arrested or have been the victim of a crime, you will want to know the rules of this procedure. If a person is released, this is called being 'granted bail'.

The Bail Act 1976 states that the accused person must be granted bail unless certain criteria apply.[7] If the offence with which the person has been charged is one for which they could be sent to prison, then the court is allowed to refuse bail if it is satisfied that there are substantial grounds for believing that if the person was given bail, even on conditions, they would do one of the following:

- fail to surrender to custody
- commit an offence while on bail
- interfere with witnesses or otherwise obstruct the course of justice, either in relation to themselves or to any other person.

In other words, if it can be demonstrated that the person is unlikely to turn up to stand trial, or that they might commit another offence if released, or that they may try and intimidate a prosecution witness, then they do not have to be released on bail.

When deciding whether to grant bail or not, the Bail Act says the court must consider, amongst other relevant matters, the following:

- the nature and seriousness of the offence and the probable sentence the person will get
- their 'character, antecedents, associations and community ties' (this means in practice that the court will look at any previous criminal record the person has, and things like whether they have a fixed address, family ties or a job)
- whether they have been on bail before, and whether they turned up at court for their trial
- the strength of the evidence against them
- whether the offence is a more serious one which could be tried in the crown court and the person is already on bail for something else when arrested
- whether there has been the time to obtain sufficient information so that a decision can be taken. If not, bail can be refused.

If the court does decide to grant bail to a person charged

with certain offences (murder, manslaughter, rape and attempting them) then the court must state the reason for that decision.[8] If the defendant has previously been convicted of homicide or rape the court must not grant bail if they are charged with such offences again unless there are exceptional circumstances which justify this.[9]

The court can release the person on bail with conditions attached. This is only permissible if it is necessary to prevent the accused running away, committing further offences or interfering with witnesses. For instance, if a man is accused of harassing a woman and she has made it clear that she fears that he will continue to do so, then a condition could be imposed that he is not to go within a certain distance of her house. Other conditions that may be attached are, for example, a condition to reside at a particular place, a condition not to contact the victim by direct or indirect means and now even a condition that the defendant must attend an interview with his legal representative.

Another condition commonly imposed is that someone must 'stand surety' for the accused person. This means that the person who agrees to stand risks losing whatever sum of money is set if the person absconds. The surety has to be suitable and the court must have regard, amongst other things, to the surety's financial resources, their character, any previous convictions, and their proximity (whether in point of kinship, place of residence or otherwise) to the person for whom they are to be surety. If you are asked to act as surety for someone then don't do it unless you are quite sure they will attend the court. You can expect little mercy if they do not and whatever sum of money you said you would risk will almost certainly be taken off you if they don't surrender to their bail and turn up at the appointed court on the appointed day.[10] If you do wish to be a surety then you will need to be able to explain to the court from where you would get the money if you are ordered to forfeit it.

Anyone who breaches their bail conditions can be arrested and brought before the court and they may not get bail again. If you are the victim and the person who has offended against you breaches a bail condition then contact the police at once and insist they arrest them.

Quite apart from the above, the court is allowed to refuse bail to the accused person if they are satisfied that they should be kept in custody for their own protection, or, in the case of persons under 18, for their own welfare.[11] This also applies even if the person is accused of a less serious offence for which they could not be sent to prison. In less serious cases, though, if the above does not apply, then the accused must be given bail unless they were given bail before and did not then turn up at court.

If the magistrates refuse to grant bail the accused person has the right to apply to a crown court judge. This application is covered by the legal aid scheme and you can be represented by your current legal team. You also have a right to apply to a High Court Judge in chambers, but legal aid is not available for this, although you can ask to be represented by an employee of the Official Solicitors Office. In certain exceptional cases, too, the prosecution can appeal to a crown court judge if they objected to bail but it was still granted.[12]

Note that there are time limits on how long a person can be held in custody awaiting trial. The rules are complicated and in this situation you should definitely ask your lawyer to advise you.

If you want to complain about a decision made about the release of someone on bail, then see Chapter 5, 'Fight Back'.

Being a Witness

Defence barristers (some of whom are women) are paid a lot of money to become skilled in putting the victim on trial, including by trawling through her irrelevant sexual, medical and other history, and engaging in the most brutal cross-examination, from which neither judge nor prosecution barrister can protect her.

Women Against Rape in an article about rape trials.[13]

She knew she could take her time to answer the questions and ask him (defence counsel) to repeat those she did not understand. She knew she could ask for a rest if she needed one.
 I think this stopped her from breaking down. I hate to think what the outcome of the case would have been if she hadn't got that preparation.

Mother of a girl aged eight who gave evidence which helped convict a teacher of indecent assault and who had first been shown a recently introduced Child Witness Pack.[14]

You may one day be asked to give evidence in court, either for the prosecution, particularly if you are a victim of a crime, or for the defence. As the above quotes demonstrate this can be a stressful business, but making some preparation beforehand can be very helpful. If you are the victim of a crime and the person who did it is caught and decides to plead guilty, you probably won't have to give evidence, but they may not make this decision until the last minute. You should be sent the Home Office leaflet 'Witness in Court' if you have been asked to go to a magistrates' court or the crown court to give evidence as a witness. This leaflet tells you what to expect. There is also a leaflet called 'Witnesses in the Crown Court', part of the Courts' Charter which sets out the standard of service which the crown courts aim to give you.[15]

Think about taking someone with you to court

If you are asked to be a witness then think about asking someone to go to the court with you. The accused person is most unlikely to be there on their own. They will probably have a lawyer with them at the very least. You could ask a friend to go with you or you could contact the organisation Victim Support (see Appendix I) which runs a witness service in all crown court centres and may also be able to help you if you have been asked to give evidence in the magistrates' court. If you are a rape victim you could also contact Women Against Rape or a rape crisis centre if there is one in your area (again, see Appendix I).

Think about visiting the court beforehand

You might also think about visiting the court where you are going to give evidence, or one like it, while a trial is going on so that you can get an idea of how it all works. You can either just go along and sit in the public gallery or you could ring the Customer Service Officer at the court concerned and ask them or the Victim Support witness service to arrange this.[16]

If you are worried about meeting the defendant

If you are particularly worried about avoiding contact with the defendant or their witnesses you should contact the Customer Service Officer at the court beforehand so that arrangements can be made to avoid you bumping into them. It is important to do this because not all courts have separate waiting areas.[17]

Other matters

The 'Statement of National Standards of Witness Care in the Criminal Justice System',[18] which 'sets national parameters for standards of service for witnesses in criminal cases', states that the courts should make every effort to arrange trial dates that are convenient to witnesses and give witnesses as much notice as possible of the date and time they are required to attend court.

There should also be provision for the special needs of witnesses, and for 'standby arrangements' (being able to wait at another location and being contacted by telephone). All witnesses should be dealt with sensitively, with regard being given to differences in language, expression, religion and customs of those from ethnic minority groups. Witnesses should be given timely information about the progress of cases and their enquiries should be dealt with promptly and helpfully. They should be given information, on request, about the outcome of cases; and expense claims submitted by witnesses should be dealt with promptly. Special arrangements should be made for witnesses at risk of intimidation, and the time witnesses are kept waiting at court should be kept to a minimum.[19]

Vulnerable witnesses

There are now special provisions for children to give their evidence through a television link in certain types of cases if the court agrees. These provisions are set out in a statute.[20] Not all courts have these facilities but if the case is in the crown court there will be a Child Witness Officer who should answer questions about what facilities are available and explain how any TV link works. As can be seen from the quote above, an information pack which aims to minimise the stress on children giving evidence in abuse cases is now available. The use of screens to prevent young children seeing, or being seen by, the defendants has also been approved in decided court cases, as has the use of screens in the case of adults, although for the latter only in the most exceptional cases.

The court layout

Most witnesses when giving evidence will find that they are in a court room which is open to the public (although the public are not admitted to youth courts). There are some helpful diagrams of the layouts and personnel in the 'Witness in Court' leaflet. You will be asked to stand in a wooden box from where you will have a clear view of the defendant and they of you. Don't be intimidated by this. You are about as safe from physical attack as you could be.

Giving evidence

You will first be asked to take the oath, ie to swear on the Bible that you will tell the truth. If you practise a religion other than Christianity you can ask to swear on that religion's 'bible' instead. If you have no religion you can ask to 'affirm'.

If you are a witness for the prosecution then the prosecution lawyer will take you through your evidence first.[21] Then comes the hard part. The defendant's lawyer (or the defendant themselves if they are not represented[22]) will then be allowed to cross-examine you. What they are supposed to do is put to you all parts of your evidence which are not agreed to by their client and to elicit from you statements which will be helpful to the defence. If things get nasty, which can happen, then what they may also try to do is to undermine your credibility with the magistrates or the jury. They can achieve this if they can show that you are being inconsistent or untruthful or are exaggerating. Various tactics could be employed with the object of confusing you. If you feel humiliated, intimidated or angry you are more likely to make a mess of your evidence. Don't let them get to you. Remember you are telling the truth and it is not you who is on trial even if it does feel like it. **You have the right to take your time and to ask for questions to be repeated if you don't understand or can't hear.**[23]

If you are a complainant in a rape case then you cannot be questioned about your past sex life unless the judge gives permission and they should not do that unless satisfied that it would be unfair to the defendant not to allow you to be questioned in this way.[24]

Publicity

You should not, unless it is necessary for evidential purposes, be required to state your address in court when you give evidence. If there is a very good reason and the court agrees, you can be permitted to write down your name instead of saying it out loud. The sort of reasons which could be taken into account are if you are a blackmail victim or if there are real grounds to fear the consequences if your identity were revealed.[25]

If you have made a complaint of rape or of other sexual offences such as indecent assault or incest, then you are entitled to anonymity unless the judge rules otherwise. Your name and address must not be published and pictures that might lead to your identification as such a victim must not be published either. The protection lasts for your lifetime.[26]

If the witness is a child or young person then the court may direct that their anonymity be preserved in a similar fashion, including not publishing the name of their school.[27]

If you have been a witness and feel that you were treated badly then you should complain, particularly if the standards set out in the Courts' Charter or in the leaflet 'Witness in Court' have not been adhered to. See Chapter 5, 'Fight Back'.

Pleading Not Guilty

If you have been charged with a criminal offence which you did not commit, you will no doubt feel outraged, intimidated or depressed, or indeed all three. Don't despair – there is a lot you can do to help yourself in this situation.

Get legal advice before you do anything

If an adult[28] is accused of committing a criminal offence, the first court they will go to is the magistrates' court. Ask a friend to go with you. You will feel much better not being on your own. Consider whether there is time to get some legal advice. If there is not, or if you are in custody and do not already have a solicitor lined up to represent you, then there will be a duty solicitor whom you can consult at the magistrates' court.[29] If you can't get yourself organised in time then ask for the case to be put off so you can go and see your chosen lawyer. The last thing you want or need is to be rushed into making a decision about whether you should plead guilty or not and whether or not you can or should ask for a jury trial.

If you later discover that you are not eligible for legal aid then look at Appendix I to see if there is any advice agency who could help you. If you do end up representing yourself look at Chapter 6, 'DIY'.

Ask for advance information

When accused of certain types of offences you have the right to be provided with what is called advance information. You should be given a notice telling you of this right. Make sure you take advantage of it. You should then be provided with copies of statements or a summary of the facts and matters on which the prosecution intend to give evidence. It helps to get this information as soon as possible, although if your case is one that is later tried in the crown court you will be served with copies of all the prosecution statements in due course.[30]

Your plea and a possible jury trial

Once you have found out exactly what you have been accused of and have obtained expert advice you will be able to decide whether or not to plead guilty. It is very important not to be rushed into this. You should never plead guilty just to get everything over with, as the implications could be very serious for you (see Chapter 4, 'Side Effects'). The magistrates will ask you to give an indication of your plea as a first step in the trial procedure, but don't commit yourself until you are sure you are doing the right thing.

Next, if the offence is one where there is a choice of court to be tried in, there will be discussions about that and you may be able to make the selection for yourself. However, some types of offence can be tried only in a particular court, be it crown or magistrates'. If you do have a choice and you choose the crown court, the jury will decide whether or not you are guilty. If you opt to be tried in the magistrates' court it will be the magistrates who will decide.

Many people feel they have a better chance of being believed by twelve ordinary people sitting on a jury than by a professional lawyer or even the lay magistrates. In the recent furore about the government's plans to limit the defendants' chance to choose jury trial[31] it has been said time and time again that black defendants often choose jury trial for this reason. There is a down side to jury trials though; there is more delay, more expense if you are paying, a more intimidating atmosphere (because there is more formality and the trial judge will be robed) and, if found guilty, possibly the risk of a more ferocious sentence. This can be a difficult decision to make so take advice before you decide.

Note that even if you are prepared to be tried in the magistrates' court, the court may decide the matter is too serious for them and the case will then be sent to the crown court. This applies even if you indicate that you are prepared to plead guilty.[32]

If the case is to be heard in the crown court then arrangements for it to be transferred there have to be made. A new procedure is being introduced whereby, if the offence is one which can only be heard in the crown court, the magistrates can send the case straight there.[33] If it's only going there because you or the prosecution want it to go there then a 'committal hearing' has to happen and if it is clear from the papers which have been served on you that the prosecution have no real evidence, you can, before the transfer takes place, ask the magistrates to stop the whole thing in its tracks.

Other pre-trial procedures and considerations

If you are tried in the crown court then you can now be compelled to give to the prosecution a 'defence statement'. This must set out the nature of your defence, matters on which you disagree with the prosecution and details of any alibi defence you intend to raise. If you fail to comply with this requirement then once again 'inferences' can be drawn at your trial.[34] If you say something at your trial which conflicts with this statement this too can be held against you. The obligation to provide this statement arises 14 days after the prosecution have disclosed material not previously shown to you which might undermine the case against you.[35] Once you have served your defence statement you should then receive any other prosecution material not previously disclosed which might be helpful in respect of your disclosed defence. You also have the right to apply to the court for further disclosure if you have reason to suspect that there is other prosecution material which should have been disclosed to you.

As explained earlier ('Silence Isn't Golden'), 'inferences' can be drawn at your trial if you have not made certain explanations at an earlier stage. Such 'inferences as appear proper' can also be drawn if you do not give evidence at your trial. This rule now applies to anyone over 10 although exceptions can be made if 'it appears to the court that the physical or mental condition of the accused makes it undesirable for him to give evidence'.[36] However, not giving evidence is not enough to convict you on its own. There must be some other evidence and you should not be convicted unless the magistrates or jury are sure beyond all reasonable doubt that you are guilty.

The trial itself

Once the actual trial takes place, whether it is in the magistrates' or the crown court, the first thing that happens is that the prosecution outline their case against you. Then they call their witnesses. 'Leading' (ie putting words into mouths) questions are not allowed. You or your lawyer will then be able to cross-examine the witness. It is important when doing so to put to the witness each bit of their evidence which you do not accept. Otherwise it will be put to you when you give evidence that you did not challenge the witness on such and such a point. The other thing you or your lawyer should be aiming to do is to get the witness to say something which could be helpful to you – for example, in a case of mistaken identity, if the answer to 'When did you last go to the opticians for an eye test, Mr. X?' is 'Twenty years ago', then that is something that you could make a point of.

All sorts of odd things come out once the live evidence begins. Whether you are represented or not it is important to write down what the witness says and underline each bit that you do not agree with or any point that you want further questions to be asked about. (Things can move so fast that this is probably all you will have time to do. When the witness has finished you can flip through your notes and the fact you have underlined something should be enough to remind you of the point you want to make.) Make sure your lawyer puts each of these points to the witness on your behalf. If you've gone to the right sort of lawyer they should check with you whether you want any points to be put before agreeing to finish their cross-examination. When you have finished, the prosecution have the right to re-examine their own witness.

If at the close of the prosecution case it could be argued that there is 'no case to answer', ie that the prosecution have failed to produce any evidence upon which you could be found guilty, then you or your lawyer are entitled to ask for the charges against you to be dismissed. Otherwise it is now your turn to put your case and call your witnesses and to give evidence yourself. If you have never been in any trouble with the police before, emphasise this and consider calling a witness to vouch for your good character. Your witnesses can also be cross-examined by the prosecution and then re-examined by you.[37]

You or your lawyer will then make a final speech. This can be very important, especially in a magistrates' court because in that court your speech will be the last word on the subject, whereas in the crown court what will happen last is that the judge will sum up to the jury.

The jury will then retire to consider their decision. (Lay magistrates may also retire to do so.) A stipendiary magistrate will probably decide on the spot.

If you are convicted you should consider lodging an appeal – see Chapter 5, 'Fight Back'.

Sentencing

If you have decided to plead guilty or if you have been found guilty then the point will come when the court has to decide what penalty to impose. If you have made it clear all along that you intend to admit the offence then that is a matter which the court must, in most cases, take into account in your favour.[38] If you are represented by a lawyer, they will make a 'speech in mitigation' on your behalf. If you are representing yourself you will be given an opportunity to speak on your own behalf to the court before you are sentenced. Whether you are represented or not, some pre-sentence preparation needs to be done.

Pre-sentence preparation

If speaking for yourself, it is always a good idea to work out in advance what you are going to say and to make a list of points to refer to, as once you are standing in the dock you may be so overcome with nerves that you find it difficult to say anything at all.

- First of all, think about the offence itself. What, if anything, can you usefully say about why you did it? For instance, if you are accused of shoplifting then there may have been some reason which led you to do something quite out of character – some unexpected financial pressure or some personal tragedy that made you very depressed and led you to take something which you did not even need. If you have been found guilty of cultivating cannabis plants then perhaps you only grew them to treat some medical condition. If you have a lawyer make sure they know your reasons for doing what you did.
- If you did co-operate with the police and readily admitted your guilt, this is always a good point to make.
- Next, consider your own personal circumstances. Have you ever been in trouble before? If not, this is a very important thing to emphasise and if the offence is one like shoplifting you can point out that you have been punished a lot just by getting a criminal record (and see Chapter 4, 'Side Effects').
- If you are likely to be fined then go through your finances carefully. The court should take everything

into account. List your gross income from all sources for the last 12 months. Then list all the deductions that have to be regularly made from it, eg tax, national insurance, pension contributions, rent, water rates, fuel bills, everything. If you have borrowed money tell them how much you still owe and how much your payments are; include hire-purchase commitments, mortgages, bank overdrafts, etc. It is most important that the court does not get the idea that you are better off than you really are. It is also worth working out how much you could afford to pay per week or month towards any fine. Don't try and get away with an offer which is ridiculously low as the court may lose sympathy with you and order you to pay your fine back at a very high rate. Don't overdo it in the other direction either and offer to pay back at a rate you really cannot afford. This could also lead to trouble.[39]

- Consider your responsibilities. Do you have dependent children, parents or anyone else that needs regular help from you? Make sure the court knows about these people and the effect on them of any sentence that may be passed.

- If you are working or looking for work consider the effect on your job or any prospective job of any sentence passed. For instance, how will not having a driving licence affect you? Would your job be held open for you if you were sent to prison and would you have much chance of getting another one if you lose it?

When the day comes

Ask a friend to come with you on the day of sentencing if possible. When considering what to wear, low-profile respectable dress is probably right. You don't want to appear too prosperous and self-satisfied but you also want to give the impression that you have dressed suitably for a serious occasion.

If you are pleading guilty a lawyer from the Crown Prosecution Service will outline the facts to the court and will give details of any previous convictions you have. If they say anything which is inaccurate or leave something out like your helpfulness to the police then, when invited to do so, as you will be, tell the court what they have got wrong and what they have left out.

When asked to speak, it is often a good idea to start off by apologising if that seems appropriate to you. Then get your list and go through the points one by one. The sorts of penalties you could be facing depend entirely on the perceived seriousness of what you have done, your past criminal record or lack of it, and your personal circumstances. This is why your list is so important. If the court does have a prison sentence in mind then they will have to warn you of this at some point, and if you are not represented they must give you the chance to have the case put off so you can get legal advice.[40] It would no doubt be a good idea to take advantage of that. See Chapter 6, 'Representation'. The court may also adjourn the case for some weeks so that a pre-sentence report can be prepared by the Probation Service. Failure to co-operate with this procedure could have serious consequences.

The sentence

The court has a number of options apart from sending you immediately to prison. It can pass what is called a suspended prison sentence, a prison sentence suspended for a specified period of time which will only be activated if you offend during that period. There are a number of non-custodial options as well, some of which can be imposed in combinations. For example:

- An absolute discharge. This is the best result. You

have no penalty except getting a criminal record.

- A conditional discharge for a given period (up to three years). Again, there is no penalty except having a criminal record, as long as you do not offend again in the given period.
- A fine. You can ask to pay this off by instalments.
- The case may be put off for a pre-sentence report to be prepared with a view to your being put on probation. This involves visiting the probation officer as and when required and there may be other provisions attached such as a condition of going for medical treatment or treatment for dependency on alcohol or drugs (your consent will be requested for the treatment aspect only).
- The case may also be put off for the court to get reports so as to consider whether you can do community service – a number of hours of unpaid work in the community.
- A Drug Treatment or Testing Order. These will be made if you are dependent on or 'have a propensity' to abuse drugs.
- Sentence can also be 'deferred' (ie, put off) for up to six months and you should be told exactly what the court expects of you during that period.
- You can also be ordered to pay compensation to the victim. If you are working and can afford to do so this can be another argument against putting you in prison immediately. It can only go in your favour if you make such an offer when you or someone on your behalf is making a speech in mitigation.

Note that if you have pleaded guilty in the magistrates' court, for certain types of offence the magistrates have the power to commit you to the crown court to be sentenced there if they consider their powers of punishment are not enough.[41]

Young offenders

The Crime and Disorder Act 1998 made numerous changes to the sentencing process for young offenders. Young offenders who did not go into custody (which is to be called a detention and training order) could already be absolutely or conditionally discharged, put under supervision of social services (similar to a probation order), or be ordered to perform community service or pay a fine. They could also be ordered to go to an attendance centre. Now, in addition, there are other non-custodial options. For instance, 'action plan orders' are being introduced. For a period of three months the young offender can be ordered to comply with a series of requirements in respect of their actions and whereabouts. The sorts of things the young offender can be asked to do are listed and include things like participating in specified activities, staying away from a particular place and complying with educational requirements. There are also 'reparation orders' (see Chapter 5, 'Fight Back' section). See also Chapter 4, 'Side Effects', which deals with the new parenting orders.

If you object to the sentence passed then you can appeal. See Chapter 5, 'Fight Back', but don't delay as there are strict time limits and your notice of appeal must be lodged within 21 days.

Victims and sentencing

If you are the victim of a crime then any 'pre-sentence report' prepared by the Probation Service should include an assessment of the effect the crime had on you. It is considered appropriate for a judge when sentencing an offender to receive information as to the impact of the offence on the victim, but if the effect is to be taken into account the judge must have actual evidence of its nature. The CPS are also under a duty to challenge the defendant's lawyer if they put forward matters in mitigation for the defendant which are untrue.[42]

In certain types of cases in the crown court, the prosecution may appeal to the Court of Appeal if the sentence is considered to be too lenient. This must be done within 28 days of the sentence being passed, and you are invited to discuss your views with the CPS if you think the sentence was too lenient.[43]

Chapter 3
In Prison

In this chapter I aim to give advice to women who do end up in prison. In the first section I give some pre-sentence advice. Then I look at the different prisoner categories, types of prison and how to obtain advice. Next I discuss the privilege system and what your entitlements to various facilities are in prison. Then I deal with the rights that women prisoners have to keep in touch with the outside world. Lastly, I look at the system of prison discipline and details of how and when you should be released.

Pre-sentence Advice

> It never occurred to me I'd go to prison. I'd left my two-year-old with my friend to come to court and the others were all at school. When I was sentenced, I had no chance to make any arrangements for them. The f—ing judge – God forgive me – he knew I had little kids but I was shipped straight to Holloway. You can't even make a phone call to your kids.
>
> Bernadette, aged 27, sent to prison for a first offence, a £136 fraud.[1]

Sometimes when you go to court you know that you might be sent to prison. But sometimes, as can be seen from the quote above, a person who is completely unprepared can be packed straight off into custody.

Take your courage in both hands and ask your lawyer, if you have one, whether there is any possibility that you might be sent to prison. If you don't have a lawyer then at least, as we pointed out in the last chapter, the court will warn you first if they are thinking of sending you to prison and they will be prepared to put the case off before sending you away. Even if you still don't want to get a lawyer, this is a chance for you to make some pre-prison plans. If your lawyer thinks there is any chance of you going to prison you should do so as well. However depressed you feel, it is best to face up to the situation and prepare for it, to whatever extent this is possible.

If you have children then you may need to make prospective arrangements for someone else to look after them if you are sent to prison, particularly if you are a single parent. If the person you choose is the father of the children and you are not married to him, then you should consider drawing up a parental responsibility agreement. Take advice about this (see Chapter 6 and Appendix I) and note the agreement should be lodged with the family court. If you choose a friend then it would be helpful to sign a letter reflecting the agreement and such factors as your authorisation for the friend to agree to any medical treatment or school trips, etc. Once again it would be a good idea to obtain advice about this. If you do nothing, then social services may have to step in. If you know of no one else who could care for your children, it might be advisable to contact social services in advance. Do not despair if social services involvement seems inevitable because this certainly does not mean that you will never get your children back.[2]

If you have elderly dependants and you cannot find

anyone else to help look after them, then you or they should take advice from an agency specialising in advising the elderly. You will find that these dependants will be entitled to some community-care services and if these are not sufficient the dependants can be cared for in residential accommodation whilst you are unavailable.

You may be worried about losing your home if you have rent or a mortgage to pay and if the place will be empty if you are sent to prison. See Chapter 4, 'Side Effects', for more detail about this but you should in any event consider taking advice about this and any other financial matters, from your local Citizens Advice Bureau for example (see Appendix I).

There are also some items you might be allowed to take into prison with you. It is therefore worth taking some things to court if you think you are about to be sent to prison. Women do not have to wear prison uniform and although toilet items will be provided (see following section) you will undoubtedly prefer things you have brought yourself. Pack a suitcase as you would if going away for a few weeks. Put in some comfortable clothes and shoes and possibly some smarter clothes to wear for visits.

Arrival

Despite scare stories of a rising tide of female violence, women still form only four per cent of the prison population, with a tiny proportion in for violent offences. Inevitably, their needs are marginalised in a male-dominated system.[3]

Information about your rights in prison

The moment may come when you are sent to a prison. Do not feel that because this has happened you have no rights at all, because that is not the case. However, some of the rights that you had when you were in the community will be taken away from you whilst you are in prison. The principal act controlling the prison system is the Prison Act 1952. This provides for rules to be drawn up for the regulation and management of prisons. For adult prisoners the most recent set of rules are the Prison Rules 1999.[4] You are entitled to see a copy of the Prison Rules and you ought also to be given a copy of something called the *Prisoners' Information Handbook*.[5]

Advice about your rights in prison

You can also obtain advice about your rights in prison. The laws about prisoners' rights are complicated and in many places in the Prison Rules phrases like 'unless the Secretary of State otherwise directs' or 'except with leave of the Secretary of State' keep creeping in. If you are in Holloway you could ask to see the Legal Aid and Bail Unit or a worker from the organisation Women in Prison. Whichever prison you are in you should be able to get help from the Citizens Advice Bureau. You could also contact the Prisoners Advice Service which has on a number of occasions helped prisoners make applications to the courts to try and enforce their rights whilst in prison. See Appendix I for details of these organisations and others which might be able to help.

Where will you go?

Which prison you are sent to ultimately will depend on the nature of your crime and how you are perceived. Adult women are either sent to a closed prison or to an open prison, the latter being prisons to which people not considered to be a risk to the public or in danger of escaping can be sent. There are only three open prisons for women.[6]

There are some prisons specifically for women (15 at the last count) but women can be kept in the same prison as men. The rules say only that 'Women prisoners shall normally be kept separate from male prisoners.'[7] You have no right to be imprisoned close to your home, but seek advice about obtaining a transfer if you are particularly disadvantaged by where you are put.

Girls aged 15 to 17 are at present sent to young offender institutions within 5 adult prisons but should not be placed in the actual adult section while waiting for their placement in the youth system.[8]

Special prisoner categories

Unconvicted prisoners

You may be detained in prison before you are found guilty of anything. This will happen if for some reason you are refused bail and is called being on remand. Unconvicted prisoners have a different status to convicted prisoners and to some extent are treated differently. For instance:

- Unconvicted prisoners must not be required to share a cell with a convicted prisoner.[9]
- An unconvicted prisoner who is prepared to pay any expense incurred may have the attendance of their own doctor or dentist if the governor is satisfied that there are 'reasonable grounds for the request'. Otherwise you will have to use the prison medical service (and see next section).[10]
- You don't have to work if you don't want to.
- You can send and receive as many letters and have as many visits as you wish, subject to limitations imposed by the Secretary of State.[11]

The good news is that if you are ultimately given an immediate sentence of imprisonment, the time you have spent on remand will be credited against this, which means you will have spent some of your prison sentence with access to privileges which will no longer be available once the sentence has been pronounced.

Contempt prisoners and fine defaulters

In the Introduction I explained that women can be sent to prison for disobeying an order in the civil courts, ie for what is called contempt of court. In Chapter 4, 'Side Effects', I will be explaining that a person who does not pay a fine can be sent to prison as well. These types of prisoner are also put into a separate category. They have the same rights as unconvicted prisoners when it comes to medical treatment, letters and visits.[12]

Reception procedures

You will be searched when you arrive and you can be searched subsequently 'as the governor thinks necessary'. You must be searched in 'as seemly a manner as is consistent with discovering anything concealed'. You must not be stripped and searched in the sight of another prisoner, or in the sight of a person of the opposite sex. This does not mean that prison staff are allowed to carry out an internal, ie intimate, search.[13]

Any cash which you have with you will be paid into an account under the control of the governor and the governor will also take into their custody articles which you are not allowed to keep.[14]

Privileges

Prison is punishment and is not for punishment. That is a very very fundamental truth which must be observed. Punishment is the deprivation of liberty. You don't add to that because that shows you have a negative attitude to the whole thing ... In a way, I think I was fortunate to find Holloway in my second week because it gave me an opportunity to say to them 'I'm sorry but I'm not going to stand for this.' Nobody should.

Sir David Ramsbotham, Chief Inspector of Prisons appointed 1 December 1995.[15]

Even though you are in prison you are entitled to certain privileges and facilities. Below and in the next section (where I concentrate on the rights to remain in contact with the outside world) I set out what you are entitled to.

The privilege system

In prison you will become subject to the privilege system which affects things like your access to your private cash and the number and quality of your visits. You will first be put into a category: 'basic', 'standard' or 'enhanced'. The governor will decide which one you start off in, but thereafter your behaviour will be assessed and the results of that assessment will decide which category you are in. The sort of thing taken into account is performance at work, relationships with other prisoners and staff, willingness to make effective use of time in custody and of course whether you have committed any disciplinary offences. Depending on which category you are in, this will affect how many privileges you get.[16] The privilege system is an important source of prison control. Any violation of prison discipline or failure to perform or demonstrate a good attitude can result in any privileges that you have being withdrawn or curtailed, even visits to you by your children. If this happens, you are supposed to be told the reason and to be given a statement about your rights of appeal.[17]

Toilet matters

You are supposed also to be provided with toilet articles which are necessary for your health and cleanliness. These should be replaced as necessary. Your hair should not be cut without your consent.[18] In practice, you will be given tampons and sanitary towels but you will probably not want to use their soap or shampoo.

Useful work

You will be able to buy your own toilet articles with wages from doing 'useful work', which you will be required to do for no more than 10 hours a day.[19] The sort of work you could be required to do is in the prison itself, such as wing cleaning or kitchen work. Outside contractors may also come in and employ you, for example to divide up colours for Lego, to put sponges into earphones or to stuff envelopes.

Food

You are supposed to eat the prison food unless the medical officer authorises you to have something else. The food is supposed to be 'wholesome, nutritious, well prepared and served, reasonably varied and sufficient in quantity'.[20] In practice, the quality of food varies but requests for special diets (eg for cultural reasons, vegetarians etc) are respected. You are not allowed alcohol, and tobacco is only allowed as a privilege.[21]

Exercise

Those over 21 are entitled to 1 hour of physical education per week. This goes up to 2 hours a week if you are under 21. If the weather permits, and subject to the need to maintain good order and discipline, you should be given the chance to spend time in the open air at least once a day for as long as the prison consider 'reasonable.'[22]

Education

Those who want them are supposed to be provided with 'reasonable facilities ... to improve their education by training by distance learning, private study or recreational classes in their spare time'. In practice, the provision of education is inconsistent and under-resourced. You could suddenly be transferred to a different prison in mid-course, which of course could be highly disruptive of your learning process. The more of an achiever you are perceived to be the more encouragement you may get, although the rules do say that 'special attention shall be paid to the education and training of prisoners with special educational needs, and if necessary they shall be taught within the hours normally allotted to work.'[23] There should be a library in each prison which you should be allowed to use[24] but what will be in them may well reflect the attitudes of the selecting librarian.

Medical treatment

As a convicted prisoner you are stuck with the prison medical service.[25] The only time you can call in a doctor of your choice is when you are involved in a court case and the doctor is needed to see you in connection with that. However, if necessary you can be taken from the prison to a hospital. Once there, if a doctor or senior nurse asks for removal of handcuffs and chains then they should be removed. If you are pregnant you are not supposed to be restrained whilst in the hospital. Whilst you are in prison, the medical officer is supposed to report to the governor if your health is likely to be affected by continued imprisonment or any conditions of imprisonment and to pay special attention to any prisoner whose mental condition 'appears to require it'.[26]

Contact with the Outside World

Prison Rule 4
(1): Special attention shall be paid to the maintenance of such relationships between a prisoner and his family as are desirable in the best interests of both.
(2): A prisoner shall be encouraged and assisted to establish and maintain such relations with persons and agencies outside prison as may, in the opinion

> *of the governor, best promote the interests of his*
> *family and his own social rehabilitation.*

Even though you are in prison you are still allowed to maintain some contact with the outside world. You have some rights to receive visits, to send letters and make telephone calls. You may even be allowed out on temporary release. If you have a baby while you are in prison you should be allowed to keep the baby with you for a period of time.

The basic position is that you are not allowed to communicate (which includes telephoning) with any outside person except where the Prison Rules permit it or as a privilege (Rule 34 (3)).

Letters

You are entitled to send and receive a letter on your arrival in prison and thereafter once a week. Additional letters are allowed as part of the privilege system. The governor or their staff will open and may read all personal letters, and may prevent them reaching you on the grounds that their contents are objectionable or that they are of inordinate length.[27]

You have an additional right to correspond with your legal adviser and any court, and those letters are only allowed to be opened if there are reasonable grounds to believe that the letter has something in it which it should not. You are entitled to be present when any such opening takes place.[28] Letters to certain organisations, eg the Prisoners Advice Service, should also remain confidential.

Visits

The basic rules for visits are as follows:

- You are allowed a visit from a relative or friend twice every four weeks. Extra visits are allowed as part of the privilege system or where necessary for your welfare or that of your family.[29] You will be given visiting orders which you must send out to your visitors. More than one person may be allowed to come but it is a good idea if the visitors telephone in advance to check how many people will be allowed in. There are now visiting centres at some prisons with waiting and play areas and a café where visitors can wait. The visit should normally take place in an open room unless special security conditions dictate otherwise.

- You may in addition be visited by your legal advisers and the prison staff may not listen to what is said.[30]
- You are not allowed to receive a visit from a person who is not a relative or friend unless the Secretary of State gives their permission. This rule can affect your contact with the media.[31]
- Your visitors may be searched but only in 'as seemly a manner as is consistent with discovering anything concealed'.[32]
- Visitors except for legal advisers may be banned on a number of bases, eg to prevent crime, for such period as is considered to be necessary. This was introduced mainly to prevent the smuggling of drugs into prisons.[33]

Telephone calls

It is possible to make telephone calls from prison. You will either be given a phone card or a pin number and you pay for the calls out of your earnings. The governor can limit the number of calls you make but should not limit those you make to your legal advisers. Calls you make to your legal advisers and to certain approved organisations should not be monitored.[34]

Temporary release

Some prisoners can be allowed temporary release. There are a number of bases on which such a release may be considered, one of which is to assist you in maintaining family ties or in your transition from prison life to freedom. Temporary release can also be granted on compassionate grounds or so that you can engage in employment or voluntary work. A risk assessment will be made before you are let out to make sure there would not be an unacceptable risk of you committing offences whilst released or of you failing to comply with any conditions imposed.[35]

Babies in prison

Prison Rule 12 (2) says 'The Secretary of State may, subject to any conditions he thinks fit, permit a woman prisoner to have her baby with her in prison, and everything necessary for the baby's maintenance and care may be provided there.' There are some mother and baby units in the prison system (at present there are four, at New Hall, Styal, Askham Grange and Holloway). These units have a nursery stocked with toys, a general association area and a sewing room. The baby should be allowed to stay with you for at least 9 months and up to 18 months, or possibly longer.[36]

If you are pregnant when you are admitted to prison then you will be assessed for your suitability for admission to a unit. If you are told you will not be admitted you should take legal advice at once. In November 1998 a woman referred to as 'Miss E' went to the High Court to challenge the decision of a multi-disciplinary admissions board, which included psychologists, probation staff and social services, that she might be disruptive in the unit and should not be admitted. The outcome was that the Prison Service agreed to hold another board and Miss E was then offered a place in a unit.

Control and Release

Control

Offences against discipline

While you are in prison you will be under their control and you can be punished if you offend against discipline. The 'offences' are listed in Prison Rule 51. They include such things as committing an assault, fighting, endangering the health and safety of others, starting fires, escaping, damaging the prison, being disrespectful to a prison officer, refusing to work or using abusive words.

It is also an offence to have taken a controlled (ie illegal) drug or to have received one during a visit. Note that you can be required to provide a urine sample which will be tested to see if you have been taking drugs. If you refuse to provide one that too is a disciplinary offence.[37] There are some defences to charges relating to controlled drugs in the rules, so make sure you take advice if you are accused of this.

Any charge should be laid as soon as possible and usually within 48 hours of the discovery of the 'offence'. You should be informed of this as soon as possible and before the governor starts to inquire into it, which should be the next day unless that is a Sunday or Bank Holiday. You are to be given a full opportunity to hear what is alleged against you and of presenting your own case.[38] If found guilty of any of these charges you can be cautioned or a number of penalties imposed, such as forfeiting your privileges for a period of up to 42 days, being excluded from associated work for up to 21 days, stoppages of earnings, cellular confinement for up to 14 days, or, more seriously, you could have extra days added to your sentence.[39]

Consider obtaining advice from Women in Prison, the

Prisoners Advice Service or the Citizens Advice Bureau if you get into trouble. See Appendix I for further details of these organisations.

Special control

The rules for 'special control' are as follows:

- Prison officers should not use force unnecessarily and if it is necessary 'no more force than is necessary shall be used'. Prison officers must not act deliberately in a way calculated to provoke a prisoner.[40]
- You can be removed from association, ie segregated, if certain criteria apply. After three days a member of the board of visitors must authorise any continuation and may do so from month to month (14 days for those under 21). The governor can decide to end this and must do so if the medical officer so advises.[41]
- You can also be placed in a close-supervision centre of a prison if certain criteria apply. This can be for up to one month but the period can be renewed on a monthly basis.[42]
- 'Refractory or violent' prisoners can be confined temporarily in a special cell but this is not to be used as a punishment and you should not be kept in there once you have stopped the behaviour in question. The governor can authorise this for up to 24 hours but if you are to be kept there longer this must be authorised by the board of visitors or the Secretary of State.[43]
- You can also be put under restraint if this is considered to be necessary to prevent you from injuring yourself or others, damaging property or creating a disturbance. The governor may order this but must immediately notify the board of visitors and the medical officer. The latter must immediately tell the governor if there are medical reasons why you should not be put under this restraint and the governor must accept this advice. This

should not be for longer than necessary nor for more than 24 hours unless specially authorised. This too is not to be used as a punishment.[44]

Release

There is not space here to go into the provisions for people sentenced to extended sentences (recently introduced for violent and sexual offences[45]), life imprisonment or 'detention at Her Majesty's Pleasure', but if you are in this situation then, again, you should seek advice from Women in Prison, the Prisoners Advice Service or the Citizens Advice Bureau.

Release on licence

The Criminal Justice Act 1991 deals with when you are entitled to be released. This statute has recently been amended by the Crime and Disorder Act 1998 and not all the amending provisions are in force at the time of writing.

When you are entitled to be let out depends partly on whether you are a short term or a long term prisoner. A short term prisoner is one who has been sentenced to less than four years. A long term prisoner is one who has been sentenced to four years or more.

You are entitled to be released on licence once you have served a certain proportion of your sentence, for instance two-thirds in the case of long term prisoners, one half in the case of short term prisoners, although provisions are being made to combine this with a curfew once the 'requisite period' has been served. Take advice when in doubt about your entitlement, particularly if you received a number of sentences at the same time. It can be quite difficult to work out exactly what your entitlement is.

If you are released 'on licence', the licence will specify the conditions you have to keep to, such as being supervised by a probation officer or having to reside at a specified address. If you do not keep to those conditions you are liable to be recalled and made to serve out the rest of your sentence.

Parole board licence

After a long term prisoner has served half of their sentence, the Secretary of State may release them on licence if recommended to do so by the parole board. The board may wish to interview you and they will consider reports made about you by prison staff. The board is supposed to include amongst its members a person who holds or has held judicial office, a psychiatrist, a person with knowledge and experience of the supervision or after-care of discharged prisoners, and a person who has made a study of the causes of delinquency or the treatment of offenders.[46] Once again, if you need help in dealing with the parole system ask for advice from the agencies mentioned above.

If as a victim you are worried about the possible release on parole of someone of whom you are frightened then you should take advice first if you wish to report your concerns to anyone in authority. A recent court case involved a woman who complained to the police that a rapist serving life imprisonment had been contacting her from prison, that he was fixated on her and she was concerned for her safety should he be granted parole. He was refused parole and he sued her for libel. Her lawyers did try and get the case stopped in its tracks but the Court of Appeal ruled that the man could proceed with his action against the woman.[47]

What you can do to prepare for your release

The rules do say that from the beginning of your sentence, consideration shall be given, in consultation with the appropriate after-care organisation, to your future and the assistance to be given to you on your release.[48]

In practice, all that may happen once you are released is that you will be given your own money back, a discharge grant and a travel warrant entitling you to travel to a particular location in the UK. It is no doubt a good idea, therefore, for you to take the initiative and do some pre-release planning yourself. If you have lost your home while you have been inside and if your children have had to be taken into care, then you should definitely seek advice from the agencies mentioned above and work with them to make some pre-release arrangement. You could also consider contacting the National Association for the Care and Resettlement of Offenders (NACRO). They run a few hostels where single people can be accommodated. You may also have the right to be re-housed by your local authority, especially if you have children or other dependants. Comprehensive advice about your re-housing rights is outside the scope of this book but there are a number of organisations which can assist you (see Appendix I).

Chapter 4
Side Effects

In this chapter I advise about the possible side effects of getting into trouble in our criminal justice system. These may be purely financial and this aspect is dealt with in the first section. Matters concerning your children, including when it is they who get into trouble and not you, are dealt with in the second section. I then look at your rights when it comes to publicity, and in the last section I look at the effects that having a criminal conviction or caution could have on, for instance, your future employment.

Financial Side Effects

If you are taken to court and found guilty of something this may well have an effect on your financial situation.

Fines

If you are fined then you can ask for time to pay. See 'Criminal Courts' section. What happens if you can't manage to keep up with the fine payments? If you do nothing about it then the court will write to you. You should make sure you read the letter carefully. It may say that unless you pay up, a 'distress warrant' will be issued addressed to the bailiffs who will be allowed to come round and take some of your property unless you then pay up in the time given. In one case a woman whose car was taken tried to argue that the court should have first looked into her finances further, but the court did not agree.[1]

What could also happen is that you will be summonsed back to the court and a 'means inquiry' will take place.[2] The court will investigate your situation, with the aim of deciding at what rate you must continue to pay off the fine. They are also likely to fix an alternative prison sentence which you will have to serve if you do not pay the fine. Remember what was said in the 'Courts' section about making sure the court knows exactly how limited your means are. It would help if you can now show that there has been a change in your circumstances which means the rate of payment should be lower. Once the hearing is over do not put your head in the sand because if you do not now pay as ordered, and an alternative prison sentence has been specified, you can then be taken straight to prison.[3]

Benefits

If you are committed to custody, whether as a convicted, unconvicted or unsentenced prisoner, it will have an immediate effect on your benefit position. The general rule is that prisoners cannot claim state benefits but there are some exceptions to this rule which you can take advantage of.

- Sentenced prisoners cannot apply for income support. Unconvicted prisoners or prisoners awaiting sentence can do so but what they are entitled to is considerably curtailed.[4]

- Prisoners cannot apply for the job seekers' allowance as they are not available for work. The same applies to prisoners on temporary release. When you are discharged from prison you can apply for the allowance again and for the first week only after your release you will not be expected to have taken any job-seeking steps.

- If you go into custody you can still claim housing benefit if your absence is only expected to be for up to 13 weeks. You are also entitled to claim housing benefit if your case has not yet been dealt with but you have been refused bail and your absence is unlikely to substantially exceed 52 weeks. (This latter right does not apply to sentenced prisoners.)[5]

- Your employer's liability to pay statutory sick pay ceases once you are taken into custody and you cannot claim statutory sick pay if on the first day of your incapacity you were in legal custody.

- If you were receiving a disability living allowance then the payment will be suspended as soon as you go into custody but will be refunded if you are not given an immediate prison sentence.

- If your partner is the one who has been sent to prison and if they have been treated as a non-dependant and your benefits have been reduced on account of this, then once they are detained you are entitled to ask for your benefits to be put back up to the full rate.

- A community care grant can be awarded to help you or your partner to care for a prisoner or a young offender on release on temporary licence.

If you are worried about losing your home because of being in prison or if you want advice about any aspect of your benefit situation then you should take advice as soon as possible from one of the agencies listed in Appendix I.

Property

Statutes now provide that the courts may make orders to confiscate property that belongs to a defendant in certain circumstances. The court must first determine whether the offender has benefited from any relevant criminal conduct.[6] If they decide they have, the court calculates how much to order them to pay. If they do not pay they can be sent to prison instead. These provisions were introduced to deal with big-time career criminals and if you are in that type of trouble you ought to have a lawyer to advise you, but make sure yourself that the financial calculations are accurate.

Criminal courts are also entitled to order a convicted person to pay compensation to the victim of the crime. See the next chapter, 'Fight Back', which details this from the victim's point of view.

If your child is found guilty of an offence then you could be ordered to pay any fine, costs or compensation which the court orders should be paid. One exception to this is where it would be unreasonable for you to be ordered to pay given the circumstances of the case.[7] In the next section I discuss parenting orders. Note that a failure to comply with one of these can result in the defaulting parent being fined.

Children

Fears of losing them

Many women are very concerned that any prosecution may result in them losing their children, or not being allowed to keep any babies they may have in the future (this is quite apart from the fact that in the vast majority of cases they will not be able to physically care for their children if imprisoned). Firstly you should not despair and assume this will automatically happen because it won't. If you are convicted of any offence of assault against, or ill-treatment of, a child, or if a child has died and you were one of the suspects (even though no one was prosecuted), then it is a fact of life that social services might be worried about you caring for that child or other children. The worst thing you can do in such a situation is to be defensive and to refuse to co-operate in any suggestion put to you. If care proceedings are taken, then see below.

Planning for a possible absence

If there is a period when you cannot care for your children because you are in prison you should try to make some arrangements as outlined in the pre-prison advice section in Chapter 3. If your children do have to go into care then they should be returned to you once you are released. If the local authority want to keep them then they will have to apply in the courts for an order permitting them to do so. Apart from other considerations, the court should not make such an order unless satisfied that this would be better for the child than making no order at all. The local authority should not even apply for such an order if alternative satisfactory arrangements can be made. Obviously if you are prepared to work with social services and co-operate with them so that your children can be properly looked after then there should be no need for care proceedings to be even started.

If you are separated or estranged from your children's father and he tries to use your problem as an excuse to take your children then you can still fight back. When considering the upbringing of a child, the law says that the child's welfare must be the paramount consideration.

There is also a welfare checklist that must be considered. This lists such principles as the need to ascertain the wishes and feelings of the child concerned in the light of their age and understanding.[8] These principles must be applied in all the situations set out above.

If you are worried at any time that you might lose your children because you have got into trouble with the criminal justice system, then seek advice immediately. Legal aid is often available on a means-tested basis. See Chapter 6.

If you are convicted of certain types of offence, it could also have implications on your being allowed to work with children in the future. Certain types of offences will also bar you from being a foster parent or adopter. See 'Reputation' section.

Children in trouble

If your child gets into trouble with the police, then this will obviously concern and affect you. Children under 10 cannot be prosecuted in the criminal courts, but child safety orders are now being piloted in some areas if a number of conditions are satisfied.[9] One of these is if the child has 'committed an act which if he had been aged 10 or over would have constituted an offence' and the child safety order is necessary to prevent a repetition. The local authority apply for the order and if one is granted the child will initially be placed under supervision. But if the child does not abide by the conditions imposed then a care order may be made instead. To some extent, the rules about when these types of care order can be made are different to the care orders discussed above. Another basis for making a child safety order is that the child has breached a ban imposed by a 'curfew notice'. Arrangements are being made so that local authorities may make local curfews banning all children under 10 from specified public areas between the hours of 9 p.m. and

6 a.m. unless they are under the effective control of a responsible person aged 18 or over.[10]

Once your child has reached the age of 10 then they can be prosecuted. If you are told that your child is in the police station then see Chapters 1 and 6, where I explain about the role of an 'appropriate adult' at a police station. Someone must act as such if the arrested person is under 17. Make sure too that your child gets legal advice. This will be free in the police station and you can use the duty solicitor if you do not have your own solicitor. If your child denies the offence then the issue of their guilt or innocence will normally be decided in a youth court and the public and press will not be allowed in. The government are putting new systems in place which will ensure that young offenders are dealt with more speedily than before.

If, having received legal advice, your child wishes to admit the offence then they do not have to be taken to court. A new system is being introduced[11] whereby the police may reprimand or warn young offenders instead of prosecuting them. Reprimands are less serious. They cannot, however, be given if your child already has a criminal conviction or has already been reprimanded or warned. There must be a realistic prospect of conviction and the child must admit that they committed the offence. The police must also be satisfied that it would not be in the public interest for your child to be prosecuted. If the above criteria apply but your child has been reprimanded already, or the police consider the offence is too serious to merit only a reprimand, then your child can instead be 'warned'. A second warning is permitted if the first one is now more than two years old. A child who is warned will be referred to a 'youth offending team' who will assess them and, if appropriate, arrange for them to participate in a rehabilitation programme.

Never let your child take advantage of this system as a

short cut when they are in fact innocent of the offence. Although being reprimanded or warned is not as bad as being convicted and getting a criminal record, there might still be adverse results later on.

If your child is prosecuted then don't despair. It does not mean that you are automatically going to lose them. I have already set out in Chapter 2 some of the non-custodial options that the court can resort to. Legal aid is available for your child and it is their means that will be assessed, not yours. It is definitely a good idea to take advantage of this because it is very important for your child to receive expert advice (and see Chapter 6). Unless your child has done something really dreadful, then it should be possible for them to remain at home as their lawyer should be able to convince the magistrates of the damaging effects of them being sent away.

Another change which is being introduced is the 'Parenting Order'.[12] If your child has been made subject to a child safety order, an anti-social-behaviour order, a sex offender order, or has been convicted of a criminal offence or if there has been a conviction relating to non-attendance at school, and if the court is satisfied that to make such an order is necessary to prevent the same thing re-occurring, the court may order you to comply with such requirements as are imposed for a period of up to 12 months and to attend for guidance and counselling sessions as directed not more than once a week for up to 3 months. If you do not comply and you have no reasonable excuse for not doing so then you can be prosecuted, convicted and fined.

Publicity

One the worst things about coming into contact with the criminal justice system is the fear that it might all get in the papers.

Adults

If you are an adult, then even before you have been convicted the press are entitled to publish the fact that you have appeared in court, your name and your address and what you have been charged with. What the press are not allowed to do is to publish anything which would interfere with the course of justice and which might lead the jury to be prejudiced against you. If the press ignore this rule they can be found to be in contempt of court themselves.[13] Once you have been found guilty then they can publish almost anything about what happened to you in court.

If you have been summoned to the magistrates' court for a criminal offence then you can be sure that somewhere at that court there will be a journalist, often from a local newspaper. They will be hoping for some juicy titbits and if you do not want your case to be reported you can only hope that, although of great importance to you, your case will be of no interest to them. In the busy metropolitan areas many courts have more than one courtroom and the journalist can't be in all of them. Unfortunately a certain amount of information-sharing goes on. Therefore, if the journalist hears that you live in a different area they may well tip off your local newspaper so that they can print the salacious details.

The worst thing you can do is to go up to the journalist and ask them not to print anything about you. That will immediately attract their interest and they will be far more likely to put your case in the papers than if you had stayed silent.

Young offenders

In the case of young people there are restrictions which forbid the press from publishing details which will lead to that person's identification.[14]

Witnesses

In the section on witnesses in Chapter 2 I gave some details about the rights of witnesses so far as publicity is concerned. The press can get into trouble if they ignore these rules. In one case the managing director of the broadsheet newspaper *Sunday Business* was convicted of the offence of publishing the name of a complainant in a rape case.[15]

Complaints

If you consider that the media have treated you unfairly then you can complain about the press to the Press Complaints Commission, 1 Salisbury Square, London EC4Y 3AE and about unfair radio or television coverage to the Broadcasting Standards Commission, 5–8 The Sanctuary, London SW1P 3JS, although the latter organisation will expect you to have first raised your complaint with the programme producer.

If something completely untrue has been published then in theory you might have a right to sue for libel, although legal aid is not available for such action. It is still worth taking advice about this, however, because in particularly blatant cases it should be possible to find a lawyer who will help you obtain compensation on a no-win-no-fee basis.

Reputation

Rehabilitation and spent convictions

If you are convicted in the criminal courts of anything other than a minor driving offence then you now have a criminal record which could affect you in the future and which could have a number of unfortunate effects. However, don't despair; the Rehabilitation of Offenders Act 1974 does provide that, to some extent, you can become rehabilitated and be able to treat the conviction as if it never existed. Such convictions are called 'spent' convictions. How long the rehabilitation period is depends upon the sentence passed and there are special rules for young offenders.[16] The rehabilitation period for adult offenders who are fined is five years; if sentenced to prison for less than six months it is seven years. For some longer sentences, ie those under 30 months, it is 10 years. If you are absolutely discharged the period is six months and for a conditional discharge it is either one year or the end of the discharge period, whichever is the longer. But for some sentences, eg ones of over 30 months, the conviction can never be spent.

Exceptions

Exempted employments

There are exceptions to the rules about spent convictions. The general rule is that when applying for a job you do not have to reveal the fact that you have a spent conviction. But when applying for certain jobs you may be given a notice telling you that the Rehabilitation of Offenders Act does not apply. In that case you will have to disclose even spent convictions. The sort of jobs in question are things like the police, traffic wardens, certain categories of social service and health service jobs and the professions such as law, medicine, accountancy and teaching.

Fostering and adoption of children

There can also be other come backs. If a person has a conviction for, or has been cautioned and has admitted, a serious sexual offence, or any offence of violence more serious than common assault or battery, then that person is disqualified from fostering a child or having a child placed with them with a view to adoption (despite the Rehabilitation of Offenders Act). A person will also be unable to foster or have a child placed for adoption if there is another person in the household over 18 of whom the same can be said.[17]

Changes in the pipeline

Part V of the Police Act 1997, which at the time of writing is not yet in force, provides that applications can be made, to what will be called the Criminal Records Bureau, for certificates which give certain information about the applicant's criminal record or the lack of it. There will be three types of certificate: a criminal conviction certificate which only specifies whether the person has any convictions which are not yet spent; a criminal record certificate, which will detail in addition whether the person has any spent convictions or cautions recorded against them (this type of certificate can only be requested if the job the person wants is one where the Rehabilitation of Offenders Act does not apply), and an enhanced criminal record certificate, where, in addition to listing convictions, spent and unspent, and cautions, any relevant matter relating to the applicant which is in central records can be included. Concern is being expressed that unproven allegations, such as matters for which the applicant was found not guilty, could be included. It is expected that job applicants and even volunteers will have to apply and pay for the appropriate type of certificate if they want a particular position. The government said in December 1998 that the scheme would be set up within two years.

Sex offenders

The Sex Offenders Act 1997 provides that anyone convicted of certain specified sex offences must now notify the police of their name, address and date of birth. If there are any changes in the name the offender is using or his address he must tell the police within 14 days. This also applies if he stays at another address for more than 14 days. If these requirements apply to the offender the judge will tell him in court when he is sentenced and the judge will also tell him for how long he must continue to register. If he is given a custodial sentence then he will be required to register with the police within 14 days of his release.[18]

Chapter 5
Fight Back

In this chapter I set out various ways in which you can fight back – obtaining compensation, or registering a protest or appeal if you feel you have got a raw deal out of the criminal justice system. In the first section I give advice about how to go about making a complaint; in the second I give some advice about private prosecutions and guidance about how to sue someone in the civil courts for damages; in the third I detail other ways by which you can obtain compensation; in the fourth I deal with inquests, judicial review and public inquiries, and in the last with your rights to appeal within the court system.

Complaints

If you are involved with the criminal system for any reason, then you could come into contact with the police, the courts, or the prison system and lawyers. It is possible to complain about all of these organisations or people. You may feel that whether this will get you anywhere is debatable and, of course, particularly for those still in prison, the fear of victimisation is bound to put you off. However, each complaint becomes a statistic and statistics can be quoted and used to embarrass those in authority who are behaving badly. You may also receive some compensation as a result of making a complaint. Therefore it is arguable that it is always worth while to complain.

Depending on who or what it is you want to complain about, there will be a different procedure for each category of person or body. Your rights to complain are now pretty extensive but when in doubt as to what to do always seek advice first. See Chapter 6, 'Advice and Representation' and also the Appendices, where some useful addresses are listed.

Police complaints

If you want to complain about the police or about something that happened at a police station, then you should definitely think about getting advice first, particularly if what has happened is serious and if you are thinking of suing the police for compensation. Any lawyer or advice agency you go to will be able to help you most effectively if you involve them at an early stage.

If you have decided to go it alone when you complain then if you are interviewed about your complaint, make sure there is someone else with you. That way, if you feel improper pressure is being put on you to forget the whole thing, there will be a witness to what has occurred.

The complaint must be made within 12 months of the incident and must relate to the conduct of a serving officer. The complaint has to be made to the relevant police force so you should write to the appropriate chief constable. Less serious complaints can be resolved informally if you agree, but if you are dissatisfied with the outcome you can still ask for a formal investigation. The formal investigation will be conducted by another police officer from a different subdivision, but if you have alleged that a police officer has caused death or serious injury then a body called the Police Complaints Authority must supervise the way in which your complaint has been handled and they may also intervene in cases where, for example, there is a public interest in the issues raised. This body was established by statute,[1] is not part of the police force and is stated to be independent of the latter. Even if the case is not one where the Authority actually supervises the investigation, if the police decide that no disciplinary charges should be brought against the officer the Authority must review that decision and may overturn it.

Once the investigation has been completed and investigated to the satisfaction of the Authority they will write to you to tell you the outcome and what action, if any, is to be taken against the relevant police officers. Actions that could be taken include prosecution, disciplinary charges or admonishments and warnings, which are normally recorded in a discipline register.

There has been a lot of cynicism about the police complaints system. An important change was made in April 1999. Previously, officers could not be disciplined if the charges could not be proved beyond reasonable doubt. Now the burden of proof has been lowered to that of 'on the balance of probabilities'.

Court complaints

If something has happened in a court which has upset you then each of the Courts' Charter leaflets has a section headed 'If you want to complain'. You are encouraged to voice your complaint to court staff on the spot, but if this does not resolve matters you can speak or write to the court manager, whose address should be displayed in the court. There is another leaflet available called 'I Want To Complain. What Do I Do?' Ultimately when you have exhausted all avenues you could complain further, via your MP, to the Ombudsman. The courts now state that you may also be able to claim compensation if you have lost money or have run up costs because of a mistake by their staff.[2]

Complaints about legal professionals

If you are unhappy about the way a judge has treated you, you should write to the Lord Chancellor at the House of Lords. Believe it or not, there is a specific procedure in place to deal with complaints about the judiciary but this will not deal with the actual decision of the judge but only complaints about the personal conduct of a judge, 'for example, that a judge was rude or offensive'.[3]

If it is the Crown Prosecution Service you want to complain about then you should write to the office which dealt with your case.[4]

If you want to complain about a solicitor you consulted and attempts to resolve it with them personally have failed, you should report the solicitor to the Law Society, which has a special section which deals with complaints called the Office for the Supervision of Solicitors. If your complaint is upheld then the solicitor may be disciplined. The ultimate sanction is for them to be struck off, ie not being allowed to practise as a solicitor any more, and you may be awarded some compensation.[5] If you want to complain about a barrister then you can write to the Professional Conduct Committee of the General Council of the Bar.[6]

There is also a Legal Services Ombudsman to whom you can complain further if you are not satisfied with the way in which your complaint against your solicitor or barrister has been handled.

Prison complaints

If you are in prison then the Prison Rules provide that you may complain to the governor and to the board of visitors. Any such complaint can be made orally or in writing, and the governor shall hear any requests and complaints that are made to him or her every day. Any such complaint may be made in confidence.[7]

There is a perception in women's prisons that making a formal complaint will lead to victimisation; also, the introduction of performance-related privileges (see Chapter 3) has stifled a lot of protest. Don't let this put you off; if you feel you have grounds for a complaint and if you are worried about how to go about it or about any come back on you, you should consider getting advice from Women in Prison or the Prisoners Advice Service. If you do get up the courage to go on with your complaint and you are not satisfied with the outcome, you can then ask for a review. There is also a Prisons Ombudsman who you can approach about some issues if you have gone through all the other procedures first but have not received satisfaction. There is a time limit of one month to do so. The Ombudsman can make recommendations and, although not all of their recommendations are necessarily accepted, the fact that some may be makes going to them worth considering.

In some cases, too, the Home Office has offered to pay compensation when prisoners' rights have been violated.[8]

Never make the mistake of assuming that the person you want to complain about is untouchable and that you will automatically be ignored if you make a complaint. That is not the case. The sort of people who treat others unfairly do so in the hope that no one will ever complain; they know that if someone does, and they are criticised, this could have serious implications for them. Police officers can be disciplined, solicitors and barristers can be struck off and even High Court Judges can be persuaded to retire.

Suing and Prosecuting

If you are unhappy about something that has happened to you within the criminal justice system, then there are certain situations where you can, as it were, take the law into your own hands and put a case before the courts yourself.

You should definitely take advice before launching into these sorts of actions as the laws about what you can and cannot sue for are complicated. There is always a risk, too, that if you lose, someone might want to claim costs against you. See Chapter 6, 'Advice and Representation', and Appendix I for guidance as to where to get help.

Private prosecutions

We have already seen that when a crime has been committed it is the duty of the Crown Prosecution Service to prosecute the suspected offender. If they refuse to do so and if a complaint (see previous section) does not resolve the situation, then you could consider launching a private prosecution. This route could be fraught with difficulty, however, because legal aid is not available and you may need to get permission from the authorities first. Make sure you get advice before doing anything. Some people have found that a better way of obtaining justice is to sue the perpetrator in the civil courts first, as a finding of liability by the civil courts might persuade the authorities that they should after all prosecute.[9]

Suing in the civil courts

Funding the action

At present, legal aid is available on a means-tested basis for many of the sorts of cases detailed below, provided the applicant has reasonable grounds for taking the proceedings and a fee-paying client would be advised to take the proceedings.[10] Legal aid can be refused if the case is not considered to be cost effective, ie if the likely costs might exceed any benefit obtained. What this means in practice is that your solicitor will usually, as a first step, obtain legal aid limited to the obtaining of a barrister's opinion and if the barrister advises that you have a reasonable prospect of success, further legal aid is more likely to be granted.[11] If legal aid is refused on the basis of the merits of the case then you can appeal against that refusal to an area committee. A notice will be sent to you explaining why legal aid was refused. See Chapter 6 for more details of the legal aid scheme.

If you are not eligible for legal aid and you are suing for damages then you may be able to find a lawyer who will take the case on a no-win-no-fee basis. If you do have to use the no-win-no-fee system you may well find that you have expenses to meet before the case is heard, such as insurance premiums (in case you lose and have to pay the costs of the opposition). You may also have to pay all the 'disbursements', ie fees for medical reports, etc. The exact extent of your liabilities to pay for things should be explained to you by the lawyer, who should also explain how much of any recovered damages will go to them if they help you win.

Suing the police

If a police officer has committed a 'civil' wrong against you, then it may be possible to sue them in the civil courts and obtain damages. Examples of the sorts of behaviour for which the civil courts have awarded compensation to a member of the public against the police are assault, trespass to land and property, false imprisonment, unlawful arrest and malicious prosecution. If false imprisonment or malicious prosecution are alleged then you have the right to ask for a jury trial in the civil court.

In a case heard in 1997 the Court of Appeal laid down guidelines as to what levels of damages should be awarded in such cases. This ended a run of decisions where larger and larger amounts were being awarded. For example, it was said that a successful claimant for wrongful arrest and imprisonment should be awarded £500 for the first hour of detention with subsequent hours being compensated on a reducing scale resulting in a total of £3000 for 24 hours.[12]

Legal aid is presently available for these sorts of cases. Because the Legal Aid Board will have to be convinced that the damages awarded are likely to justify the amount being spent, it may be difficult to get it given the cost of jury trials and the expected level of awards.

In the past, where the police have been sued for negligence, for example for not arresting a person for a crime and thereby causing injury to another, they have managed to avoid liability because the courts have held that they could not be sued on this basis. The mother of one of the victims of the Yorkshire Ripper, for instance, failed in her attempt to sue the police for damages.[13] However, when the father of a 15-year-old boy was killed by a teacher who had developed an unhealthy obsession for him, the boy and his mother won some redress in the European Court of Human Rights, who found that a breach of Article 6 (1) (which deals with the right to a fair hearing) had occurred. Each of the applicants was awarded £10,000.[14] It is definitely worth taking advice, then, about your chances, if you believe you have a claim against the police for negligence in failing to carry out their duties to you or your family.

Suing other people

Unjustified behaviour by store detectives can also enable a person to sue for damages. In one case a woman bought some chicken pieces at a local butcher's and placed them under her daughter's pram. She then ventured into a supermarket. A store detective from the latter stopped her outside, accused her of stealing the chicken from the supermarket and made her empty the contents of her pram in front of other shoppers and passers-by. In the end the store detective did accept the woman's explanation but the woman was later awarded £750 damages for false imprisonment and slander.[15]

Prisoners may be able to sue for damages if, for example, a woman is detained in prison for longer than she should be. The Prison Service may be prepared to offer compensation where it is recognised that a prisoner has been wrongly treated.[16]

As mentioned above, you can also consider suing a person who has committed a crime against you in the civil courts for damages. From a purely financial point of view this is definitely not worth doing unless the proposed defendant has some assets which can be used to satisfy any judgement and costs awarded against them. In one case a wife sued her husband for rape after a decision had been made that he should not be prosecuted. She was awarded £14,000 damages in the civil court.[17] A teenager successfully sued her former step-father for sexual abuse and was awarded £50,000.[18] A woman who felt too devastated to contact the police instead sued her former boss in the civil courts for damages for rape and was awarded £74,000. In that case the man appealed to the Court of Appeal where he lost and was ordered to pay costs estimated at £95,000.[19]

Note that if you have successfully obtained damages from the Criminal Injuries Compensation Agency (see next section) you will be expected to pay them back out of any damages you recover in the civil courts.

The incorporation of the European Convention on Human Rights into our law (when this comes into force) should make it much easier for anyone who comes into conflict with our criminal system to obtain redress. Right to life, liberty and security of person, the right not to be subjected to torture or to inhuman or degrading treatment or punishment, the right to a fair trial (see above) and freedom of expression, are examples of some of the principles which the Convention upholds and the incorporation will mean that our courts will have to apply these principles.

Compensation

If you wish to claim compensation for something that has happened to you, there are a number of avenues that you can take.

Financial compensation via the criminal courts

If you have been the victim of a crime and someone is prosecuted and found guilty of that crime, then that person can be ordered by the criminal court to pay compensation via the court to you.[20] Compensation can be ordered for any personal injury, loss or damage resulting from the offence, in such amount as the court considers appropriate, considering the evidence and any representations made to the court on behalf of the accused or the prosecutor. The court must also take into account the means of the offender. One advantage to you of this system is that the criminal court takes on the responsibility for enforcing the payment and the offender can end up in prison if they do not pay up. You may find that the money is paid to you by instalments and this will happen if the offender cannot afford to pay you back all at once. If you want to be compensated by this method then make sure the Crown Prosecution Service knows that you wish to make this claim.

Reparation from young offenders

Arrangements are being made so that people between the ages of 10 and 17 who have been convicted of a criminal offence can, in certain circumstances, be made subject to a 'reparation order'. The reparation may have to be made to the victim of the crime, or a person affected by it or to the community at large. The offender cannot be ordered to work for more than 24 hours or to make reparation to a person unless that person consents. The reparation is to be performed under supervision and within three months of the order being made.[21]

Compensation from the CICA

Another way that victims of crimes of violence (only) can obtain compensation is via the Criminal Injuries Compensation Scheme. You must be able to show that you have been physically or mentally injured as a result of being a victim of a crime of violence.[22] However, it is not essential that anyone has been arrested, prosecuted or found guilty of the crime. You have to establish that this has happened on the balance of probabilities only.[23] You may claim on behalf of yourself or your child. You can also claim if you qualify as 'a dependant or relative' of a victim of violence who has since died. The injury must be serious enough to qualify for the lowest level of award (at present £1000). There are time limits and you must make sure the Criminal Injuries Compensation Agency receive your application within two years of the date of the incident. If for some reason you are out of time it is always worth seeing if an exception can be made, because this is possible in certain circumstances.[24]

To make the claim, obtain a form from the CICA.[25] It is worth checking with them first which sort of form you need and also make sure they send you their explanatory booklet. When you have filled out the form keep a copy of it for future reference. The CICA should acknowledge receipt and give you a reference number. If you don't hear back, chase them up. They will then make enquiries of the police, and the medical and other relevant authorities. You will have been asked on the form to consent to this. You may be asked to attend to be examined by a doctor nominated by the CICA.

Once all the enquiries have been made, which may take some time, the CICA will then write and tell you whether they are prepared to make you an offer of compensation and if so how much. The calculation of the compensation is now based on a tariff system,[26] mostly at present with different levels attracting different levels of compensation, the bigger the number the bigger the award. For example, under the category 'head' and 'teeth', loss of one front tooth is put at level 3 and attracts an award of £1500. Under the category 'lower limbs', a sprained ankle that is disabling for more than 13 weeks is put at level 6 and attracts £2500. A disabling mental disorder, confirmed by psychiatric diagnosis, lasting over 28 weeks to 1 year is put at level 9, which awards £4000. Non-consensual vaginal and/or anal intercourse is put at level 12 and you get £7500. There are also some provisions for claiming loss of earnings if you are likely to lose more than 28 weeks' worth, and after 28 weeks some special expenses can be paid.

If compensation is refused, the CICA must tell you why. They have a discretion to refuse if, without good reason, you did not report the crime to the police as soon as possible and if you have not been helpful in the prosecution process. The award can also be blocked because of your alleged conduct, eg if you agreed to take part in a fight or if you were injured while attempting to obtain revenge against the assailant. You can also be refused on the basis of your character. However, helped by the English Collective of Prostitutes and Women Against Rape,[27] prostitutes have been awarded compensation for being raped. There are also provisions to prevent the perpetrator from benefiting, so if you are still living with a man who assaulted you compensation will be refused, and in cases of violence against co-habitees a prosecution must have taken place unless there is some good reason why not.

If you do not wish to accept their offer or lack of it then you can ask for a review within 90 days. If you do not wish to accept the review then you can appeal within 30 days to the Criminal Injuries Compensation Appeals panel. You can ask for an oral hearing where you can put your arguments for an award that you feel is appropriate. If you are dissatisfied with the results of that appeal then it may be possible to challenge the result in the High Court by means of judicial review.[28] Legal aid is not available for representation at a CICA panel hearing. However, if your means are low enough you can use the 'Advice and Representation' legal aid scheme to consult with a lawyer and get help with filling out the form and corresponding with the CICA. The lawyer could also help prepare written submissions for any oral hearing. If a judicial review is needed then legal aid is available for that on a means-tested basis.

If you are not eligible for legal aid and if you can't afford legal advice, don't let that put you off because the CICA scheme is intended to be user friendly. However, if a high value claim is being made[29] it is always advisable to get expert advice, even if you do have to pay, as you may be offered an amount which is far lower than you are entitled to if you go it alone.

There are a number of organisations who will help you if you are not eligible for legal aid – see Appendix I.

Compensation for wrongful conviction

The law says that compensation can be paid to those who have suffered punishment as a result of a wrongful conviction. The conviction must have been reversed or a pardon granted, and the Home Secretary must be sure beyond reasonable doubt that there has been a miscarriage of justice. The compensation is decided by an assessor appointed by the Secretary of State.[30]

Enquiries

In certain circumstances, some sort of judicial or public inquiry may take place following events which have occurred in the realm of the criminal law.

Inquests

If someone has died, an inquest will sometimes be held to determine how, when and where that person died. If the coroner receives information that a person in their area has died a violent or unnatural death or a sudden death of which the cause is unknown or has died in prison, then they should ensure that an inquest into the death is held.[31] If a person dies in police custody an inquest should, in most cases, also be held. Sometimes a jury is convened to bring in the verdict. This will happen if the death was in prison or police custody or is alleged to be as a result of the actions of the police purportedly in the exercise of their duties. An inquest is unlike other court cases in that the coroner is in charge of it and arranges for witnesses to be called, and it is the coroner who first questions all the witnesses. When he or she has finished then certain people[32] are allowed to question the witnesses as well but the coroner is allowed to disallow any question which in their opinion is not relevant or is not a 'proper' question.

At the end of the inquest the jury or the coroner give their verdict on who the deceased was and how and when they came by their death. The sorts of verdict that can be returned are 'death from natural causes', suicide, accident or misadventure, lawful or unlawful killing, or an open verdict if the cause of death is still uncertain.

If someone you care about has died and you suspect that something has gone on in a prison or a police station which should not have gone on, and you want to do something about this, and/or to claim compensation for yourself or your dependants, it is very important that you attend any inquest held and if possible get legal representation. This is because facts may come out at the inquest which will be vital to any later action you wish to take, and there is always the possibility that the coroner may make some announcement which might help prevent the same thing happening again.[33]

Legal aid is presently not usually available for representation at an inquest hearing[34] but you can contact the organisation Inquest (see Appendix I) as they offer a free legal and advice service on inquest procedure to the bereaved. There are also lawyers who are prepared to act for free for bereaved relatives and Inquest could help you get in touch with one of them. You should now be provided in most cases with copies of relevant documents before the inquest takes place, such as statements of witnesses and of the post-mortem report.[35]

Judicial review

If you are not satisfied with the outcome of the inquest or the way it was conducted then one way of challenging it is to apply in the civil courts for 'judicial review'. Judicial review is a procedure that can sometimes be used as a method of challenging some of the unfair things that go on in police stations, prisons and courts. An unfair decision of the Criminal Injuries Compensation Agency might be challenged by this method as well, and if the Crown Prosecution Service have not prosecuted someone when they should have done, this too can be the subject of a judicial review application. The CPS was challenged via judicial review in two cases where they did not prosecute police officers, after inquest juries had returned verdicts of unlawful killing regarding two men who died in police custody.[36] The CPS conceded they were wrong before the court got round to making a decision.

Legal aid is presently available in respect of judicial reviews. However, this is a very technical legal area and you should definitely get some legal advice before considering it (see Chapter 6). Also note there is a time limit within which you should apply – three months from when the relevant decision is made. Anyone who tries to apply outside this time limit will have a hard job justifying the delay and the application may be blocked on the grounds that you have left it too late.

Public Inquiries

In exceptional cases the government can decide to hold a Public Inquiry into past events.[37] This happened in the case of Stephen Lawrence, the murdered black teenager, after a long struggle by his parents. The report of Sir William McPherson, who conducted the Inquiry, was published on 24 February 1999 and contained 70 separate recommendations. The government then published an action plan setting out their response to the report and they have accepted and are prepared to act on some of the recommendations. For instance, they have accepted Recommendation 11, that the full force of race-relations legislation should apply to all police officers, and Recommendation 33, that in respect of racist crimes the Crown Prosecution Service should, when weighing up whether to prosecute someone or not, consider that if the evidential test is satisfied there should be a rebuttable presumption that it is in the public interest for a prosecution to take place.[38] Some of the inquiry recommendations are already being acted on to some extent.[39] Stephen Lawrence's parents have achieved a great deal for other people and they themselves have now issued High Court writs claiming damages from the five men suspected of killing their son and the Metropolitan Police Commissioner.[40]

Appeals

If you wish to challenge the fact that you have been found guilty of something, or if you feel you have been sentenced too harshly and you wish to apply to have the sentence reduced, then you should consider lodging an appeal. But don't delay, because there are time limits. Also you should note that you will not be able to refer your case to the Criminal Cases Review Commission (see below) if you have not exhausted your right to appeal first.

Magistrates' court

If you were tried and/or sentenced at a magistrate's court then in most cases you will have to appeal to the next court up which is the crown court. You have 21 days in which to fill out the necessary form which you can get from the court's office. The appeal takes the form of a re-hearing, so there is always the risk that you will end up with a worse sentence than you got in the first place. It would be a good idea, therefore, to get some advice before launching into this. There is another way of challenging a magistrates' court decision in respect of a point of law only (as opposed to fact). This is called appealing by way of 'case stated' to the divisional court and once again there is a 21-day time limit. As mentioned previously, it is sometimes possible to apply also for judicial review, if, for example, there has been some procedural irregularity. However, both the latter procedures can get pretty complicated and you should definitely get advice before launching into either. If your case took place in the magistrates' court then you may have been sentenced in your absence. This often happens with driving offences. If you can establish that an injustice has taken place then you may be able to persuade the court to alter or set aside the sentence, if you can convince them that it would be in the interests of justice to do so.[41]

Crown court

If you were tried in the crown court and were convicted by a jury then you will need leave from a single judge to apply to the Court of Appeal (Criminal Division) if you wish to set the conviction aside. The time limit is 28 days. You can still carry on even if leave is not granted (the time limit is then 14 days), but you will probably not get legal aid and there are other risks attached.[42] The law says that the Court of Appeal 'shall allow an appeal against conviction if they think that the conviction is unsafe'.[43]

Court of Appeal

Appeals from the Court of Appeal go with leave (which can be granted if a point of law of general public importance is involved or if the point of law is one which the House of Lords ought to consider) to the House of Lords. It is also possible from there to apply to the European Court of Human Rights via the European Commission on Human Rights if you are advised that a violation of the European Convention on Human Rights has occurred. You must first have exhausted all your domestic remedies and the whole process can take two to three years. Once the incorporation of the Convention into our domestic law comes into force then hopefully there will not be the need for as many cases to be taken to Europe as has happened in the past.

If you had legal aid before you were convicted and sentenced then this will cover you being advised about whether you should appeal and where appropriate preparing the necessary notices. To get legal aid for the actual hearing you will have to apply further and support from your legal advisers is crucial to ensure that the legal aid continues.

In Chapter 2 I mentioned that in certain circumstances the prosecution has the right to appeal to the Court of

Appeal if they consider that a sentence passed is unduly lenient.[44]

Criminal Cases Review Commission

In certain circumstances it may be possible to refer your case to the Criminal Cases Review Commission which has been set up to investigate miscarriages of justice. The Commission may review any conviction or sentence passed by magistrates' or crown courts. The Commission can then refer cases back to the crown court or Court of Appeal where the matter will be treated as if a further appeal is taking place. The Commission will only consider referring a conviction back if there is a real possibility of winning the appeal because there is an argument or evidence which was not presented before, or some other exceptional circumstance justifying the reference back. In the case of sentences there must be an argument on a point of law not previously raised or some new information not previously given. If the Commission decide not to refer your case back they should write explaining why and give you a further opportunity to comment. You can obtain an application form from the Commission,[45] and legal aid is available but only via the Advice and Representation scheme (see Chapter 6). The Commission, which was only set up in 1997, has been inundated with applications and at the time of writing there is unfortunately such a backlog of cases that applications might not be investigated for up to two and a half years.

Another role of the Commission is to refer cases to the Home Secretary where it feels a royal pardon should be considered. The case of Helen Duncan, the last woman to be jailed under the Witchcraft Act 1735, is one where the Home Secretary has been asked to consider recommending to the Queen that a posthumous pardon be granted. Ms Duncan was sent to prison during the Second World War for 'pretending to raise the spirits of the dead'.[46]

Chapter 6
Advice and Representation

In this chapter I give advice about lawyers and duty solicitors and I also give some explanation about the legal aid system. In the next section I give further guidance about how to represent yourself and in the last section I explain the rules about acting as an 'appropriate adult' in a police station.

Legal Aid and Lawyers

Lawyers

Barristers and solicitors

If you are accused of a crime or if you have been a victim of one, you may wish to obtain legal advice about your situation from a qualified lawyer. In this country practising lawyers are either solicitors or barristers. At present you cannot obtain access to a barrister unless you first consult a solicitor who then refers your case to one. At one time, only barristers were allowed to act as advocates in certain types of court, but solicitors who have obtained a special qualification can now do so as well. A barrister is probably best regarded now as a specialist lawyer called in where the case is serious or complex (but solicitors sometimes do use barristers to deputise for them if they are too busy to attend all their court hearings).

Making the selection

The first step for you is to find a solicitor who will be able to deal properly with your particular type of problem. Do not just look up the nearest one in *Yellow Pages*. Nearly all solicitors specialise in particular areas these days and you need one who is skilled in dealing with your particular type of problem. For certain types of cases the Law Society have specialist panels of solicitors who have demonstrated that they have the right types of skills to conduct the matter in question.[1] You should consider taking advice about your choice of solicitor from one of the agencies listed in Appendix I. You may also find that one of your friends has had a problem similar to your own and can recommend someone to you. It is one of the jobs of the solicitor to select the right sort of barrister for you so you do not need to worry about that, but if you know of a barrister who you would like to speak for you then don't be shy to discuss this with your solicitor.

If you become concerned at any time about whether the solicitor you have consulted is any good then it may be advisable to change to another one. Take advice first, as this could be expensive if you are paying privately and if you are on legal aid then the Legal Aid Board will have to agree to the change. Don't leave things as they are, though, as you do have the right to be represented properly. You also have the right to complain about lawyers (see Chapter 5, 'Fight Back').

Information about cost

You may be worried about how much this will cost. Don't panic; you may well be eligible for legal aid (see later paragraphs) and any solicitor you consult is under a duty to advise you about the availability of legal aid in your case. You may find that you will be asked to contribute towards the costs of legal aid representation and the solicitor must advise you about that too before you commit yourself to that expenditure.

If you are claiming damages or compensation then another thing which the solicitor must warn you about is the effect of the 'legal aid statutory charge'. This is the system whereby the Legal Aid Board is entitled to deduct from the money you recovered any charges outstanding in respect of your legal costs. In some civil cases hopefully the defendant will have paid all of them and you will lose nothing but if you are claiming from the CICA, for instance, that will not be the case.

If you are not eligible for legal aid then the solicitor must give you accurate information about how much it will cost to consult with them.

At present, any solicitor who is prepared to do legal aid work is allowed to do so but there are plans to allow only solicitors who are approved by the Legal Aid Board and have a legal aid franchise and a contract to represent anyone who needs legal aid.

Duty solicitors

If you have been arrested and taken to the police station, or if you have been asked to attend a police station to be questioned about your alleged involvement in some criminal activity, then you are entitled to have free legal advice via the legal aid scheme. This is one situation where you will not be means-tested. You are entitled to have the solicitor of your choice (preferable if you have been able to select one already) or the duty solicitor. The latter is a solicitor who has been specially approved by a local duty solicitor committee, who should not admit any solicitor onto the list who does not know what they are doing. They are allowed to send a para-legal, who is not a solicitor, but that person must be what is called 'accredited'.

If you have been ordered to attend at a magistrates' court then there will usually be a duty solicitor scheme there which you may well wish to take advantage of if there has not been time for you to consult with your chosen solicitor. This service is also free via the legal aid scheme. The duty solicitor (this person will definitely be a solicitor) can provide you with initial advice about things like applying for legal aid or for an adjournment to obtain advice from your regular solicitor, and, if you have arrived at the court in custody, they can apply for bail for you. The duty solicitor can also assist you if you are in court as a result of a failure to pay a fine or other sum, or for a failure to obey an order of the court, where such failure may lead to imprisonment.[2]

If you are really desperate to get it all over with at once and are sure that you should plead guilty, the duty solicitor can speak for you if necessary. You may find, however, that the duty solicitor at your court is far too busy to be able to give your case the consideration it merits. In that case it may well be best to ask the duty solicitor to help you get the case put off to another day so you can consult with them or your chosen solicitor when there is more time.[3]

Legal aid

Advice and representation

Apart from the situations set out above, legal aid is means-tested. There are various types of legal aid: first there is the Advice and Representation scheme, under which those who pass the means test may receive free legal advice about any question of English law. The scheme covers general advice, letter writing, negotiating, obtaining a barrister's opinion and preparing a written case to a tribunal (which includes the CICA). What the scheme does not cover is representation in a court or tribunal. The solicitor can do a basic two hours' worth of work to start with and if more help is needed special permission to exceed this limit must be obtained from the Legal Aid Board, who will ask your solicitor to justify this expenditure in every respect. The means test for this scheme is now *very* mean. If you are on income support you will qualify unless your savings are above the set limit, which at present is, for instance, £1000 if you are a single person with no dependants. Otherwise you may be assessed as having to pay a contribution or you may not be eligible at all. However, some solicitors may be prepared to give you the initial advice for nothing, especially if they realise that you will get legal aid in the end.

Legal aid certificates

If you want to be represented in a criminal court or if you want to sue someone else in a civil court then you, with the help of your solicitor, will have to apply for what is called a legal aid certificate. There are two criteria you must fulfil to get one of these: the merits test and the means test.

The merits test

If you want to be represented in a criminal court the 'merits test' means that it must be in the interests of justice for you to get legal aid.[4] You will usually have to establish one of the following:

- That the offence is such that if proved it is likely that the court would impose a sentence which would deprive you of your liberty[5]

- or will lead to loss of your livelihood or serious damage to your reputation
- or that the determination of the case may involve consideration of a substantial question of law
- or that you may be unable to understand the proceedings or to state your own case because of your inadequate knowledge of English, mental illness or other mental or physical disability
- or that the nature of the defence is such as to involve the tracing and interviewing of witnesses or expert cross-examination of a witness for the prosecution
- or that it is in the interests of someone other than the accused that the accused be represented (this would apply in, eg, a rape allegation where it would be better for the victim not to be cross-examined by the accused).

Some defendants have to be granted legal aid (unless they could obviously pay their own legal costs), eg those committed to the crown court on a murder charge, but for most people the above are the criteria which apply. The application for legal aid is considered by the court where you are appearing. If you are refused it on the grounds of the interest of justice, you may have a right of appeal to an area committee of the Legal Aid Board. The court have to write to you telling you why your application has been refused and in that notice they must also tell you if you have such a right of appeal.

If you wish to sue someone else in the civil court then different criteria apply to the granting of legal aid and no-win-no-fee schemes are being introduced. Both subjects are discussed in Chapter 5, 'Fight Back', 'Suing and Prosecuting'.

The means test
When it comes to means, exhaustive questions will be asked about your income, capital and about the means of

those close to you. You will have to provide extensive documentation. Your solicitor will help you fill out the relevant form. You may be assessed as having to pay a contribution towards your legal aid which you can do by instalments. If you are later acquitted or if you win the case you may get this money back. You can't actually appeal to the area committee about a refusal of legal aid on means grounds but if a mistake has been made in the assessment or if your means later change for the worse then refusal on this ground can be reconsidered.

What legal aid covers in the criminal courts

If legal aid is granted in the criminal court then it covers the cost of a solicitor to prepare your defence before you go to court and to represent you there. If the case requires a barrister, particularly if it is to be heard in the crown court, that may also be covered. This means that while your case is in the magistrates' court you may not be allowed to have a barrister unless it is considered to be serious enough. Criminal legal aid can also cover advice about an appeal (see Chapter 5, 'Fight Back', 'Appeals') and it will also cover an application for bail (including to the crown court in the case of magistrates' court proceeding). As already mentioned, legal aid is not available to bring a private prosecution.

DIY

If for some reason you cannot get legal aid and you end up having to represent yourself, don't be intimidated. A lot of people do represent themselves and they do remarkably well. Michael Randle represented himself when accused of assisting in the escape from prison of Soviet spy George Blake. He was acquitted and has written a book called *How to Defend Yourself in Court*.[6]

Firstly, you have a right to represent yourself. This fact has caused problems in some rape trials where the accused man has taken advantage of this right to personally cross-examine the victim. The government does plan to take this right away from people accused of rape but there are no plans to stop those accused of other crimes from being allowed to represent themselves.

A person who is not a qualified lawyer is not allowed to represent you in a criminal court (lay representatives are only allowed for small claims in a civil court), but what you are allowed to do is to have someone with you in court to help you. The person will not be allowed to address the court on your behalf and will be expected to sit quietly and offer help only, but that can be amazingly supportive and you should definitely take advantage of this right. Such a person is called a 'McKenzie adviser'.[7]

Most people who do represent themselves in a criminal trial do so in the magistrates' court. This is because legal aid is far more widely available in the crown court. Whichever court you are representing yourself in you should look at Chapter 2, 'In the Criminal Courts'.

If you plead guilty, the court will want to proceed there and then. See the sentencing section of Chapter 2 for tips as to what is likely to happen and how to handle things. If you want someone to say what a good person you are then the court should allow this but the person will be expected to give evidence from the witness box. As pointed out above, they cannot actually represent you unless they are a lawyer.

If you are pleading not guilty and the case is to be heard in the magistrates' court then once you have told the court that you are pleading not guilty they will put the case off to another date and will set aside some time for it. If they try and fix it on a date when one of your witnesses will be unavailable for a good reason then point this out and ask for another date. Make sure you have asked your witnesses about their future availability before you go to court to plead not guilty. If you have chosen jury trial then the case will also be put off to another date so it can be transferred to the crown court.

There are a number of pre-trial preparations that need to be done if you wish to plead not guilty, whichever court you are appearing in. As soon as possible contact anyone who witnessed what happened and ask them if they will give evidence for you. If they say yes then take a statement from them and ask them to sign it. Also write out your own statement. It is amazing how quickly you may forget what actually happened. If someone refuses to act as witness you can consider asking the court to order them to attend the hearing by the issue of a witness summons. You should think carefully before doing this though, as the fact that you have forced the person to attend may cause them to become hostile to you and this may not be terribly helpful. You should try and find the time to go to a court like the one you will be appearing in and observe what is going on so you can get a feel of things. This will also be helpful even if you intend to plead guilty.

It is also worth visiting your local reference library and seeing what useful books there are. Knowing the law about the crime with which you are charged is very important and knowing as much as possible about court procedures is also helpful. Most reference libraries have a three-volume light blue tome called *Stones Justices Manual*, which sets out the laws in the magistrates' court. The statutes and decided cases which affect the offence with which you are being charged will almost definitely be set out there unless you are accused of violating a local bye-law. The *Manual* also contains useful information about procedure and sentencing in the magistrates' courts. Look in the Index for the subject you want and it should direct you to the right place. If you are being tried in the crown court the equivalent manual is called *Archbold*, a large red book with a separate Index. This may be more difficult to find.

Your library may also have a large legal encyclopedia called *Halsbury's Laws*. This contains details of the law on just about everything. For instance, there are sections about the criminal law, the police, prisons, magistrates and many other subjects only touched on in this book. There is a separate encylopedia called *Halsbury's Statutes* which has the text of many statutes in it. Additionally, your library may have some text books about the criminal law and procedure.

If there is something you want but can't find then it is always worth asking the librarian if the material is available. The library may have a complete set of statutes, statutory instruments, local bye-laws and law reports which they may keep at the back.[8]

Make sure you get copies of the prosecution statements. If these have not been given to you via advance information then ask the Crown Prosecution Service to provide them anyway and complain if they are not helpful. Go through the statements carefully and make a list of all the questions you wish to put to the prosecution's witnesses based on what you see in their statements. Look at the 'Not Guilty' section of Chapter 2 for advice about what cross-examination is supposed to achieve. Other things will come out when the witness gives evidence but if you have taken the advice in Chapter 2 to note down what the witness says and underline everything that is worth raising further questions about, then you will be well placed to cross-examine the witness about these extra points.

Also prepare, to the extent this is possible, for your final speech. Don't forget, too, that once the prosecution case has finished then you can ask for the charges against you to be dismissed at that point if no evidence has been put before the court which could lead to your being convicted. If the case does proceed and you do have to make that final speech then the points you must raise are these:

- Your good character if you have never been in trouble before. Very important if your credibility is a central issue.
- Legal arguments if your research in the library has produced something helpful and you can show that the prosecution have not produced any credible evidence to found a conviction for the offence you are charged with.
- Factual arguments to show that the prosecution's case is flawed. List all the strong points in your own case and all the weak points and discrepancies in theirs.
- The prosecution must prove the charges against you beyond all reasonable doubt and if there is any doubt at all of your guilt, you are entitled to be found not guilty. Emphasise this fact right at the end and ask the court to acquit you.

If despite your best efforts you are still found guilty and/or you are given a sentence that is too severe, then consider appealing (see 'Appeals' section). Don't forget there is a 21-day time limit in the magistrates' court and take advice first. See Appendix I.

Appropriate Adults

In the section on police stations I have already referred to the Codes of Practice. These make provision for the protection of 'vulnerable suspects'. Those deemed to be vulnerable are 'juveniles' (those appearing to be under 17) and mentally disabled people. The Codes refer to people suffering from mental disorder as defined in the Mental Health Act 1983. In practice, this covers those suffering from mental illness or with learning difficulties.[9] When someone in these categories ends up in a police station then a person referred to as an 'appropriate adult' should be found to assist.

If the vulnerable suspect is a juvenile then the person called for should firstly be their parent or guardian or, if they are in care, the care authority or voluntary organisation. If the juvenile is estranged from his parents and does not want them to be the appropriate adult then that wish should be respected. If none of these are available a social worker can be asked to come (however, a social worker to whom the juvenile has admitted committing the offence should not be the appropriate adult). Failing that, a responsible adult of 18 or over who is not a police officer or employed by the police can be brought in.[10]

If the suspect is mentally disabled then the appropriate adult can be a relative, a guardian appointed under the Mental Health Act 1983 or some other person responsible for the person's care or custody. Failing that someone who has experience of dealing with mentally disordered or mentally handicapped people can be called on but this person must not be a police officer or employed by the police. Social workers who have experience in working with mentally disabled people often get asked to help. If none of these are available then some other responsible adult aged 18 or over who is not a police officer or employed by the police can be called on.

The Codes say that in the case of mentally disabled people it may in certain circumstances be more satisfactory for all concerned if the appropriate adult is someone who has experience or training in their care rather than a relative lacking such qualifications. But if the person prefers a relative to a better qualified stranger or objects to a particular person as the appropriate adult, their wishes should, if practicable, be respected.

If a juvenile is arrested the custody officer must, if it is practicable, find out who is responsible for their welfare. That person must be informed as soon as possible that the juvenile has been arrested, why they have been arrested and where they are detained. Even if the juvenile is in care the Codes say the police should consider informing parents as well as the care authority. In the case of all vulnerable suspects the police must as soon as possible inform the appropriate adult of the grounds for detention and ask the adult to come to the police station to see the person.

If you are an 'appropriate adult'

The Codes make numerous references to the role of the appropriate adult. If you are acting as one, you are allowed to inspect the custody record on arrival at the police station and even if the person has already been told of their rights this must be repeated in your presence and a notice of it must be given to you. Even if the suspect has been cautioned already the caution must be repeated in front of you and reprimands and warnings (in the case of young offenders) must be given in your presence. The suspect should not be interviewed or asked to provide or sign a written statement if you are not there, unless certain exceptional circumstances apply. If you are present at an interview the police should tell you that you are not expected to act simply as an observer; that the purpose of your presence is first to advise the person being questioned and to observe whether or not the interview is being conducted properly and fairly, and second, to facilitate communication with the person being interviewed. If the suspect is charged this must be done in your presence and the notice about it and the warnings about the risk of remaining silent are to be given to you. If a decision is made to detain the suspect then you may make representations on their behalf. There are also provisions for the appropriate adult to be present when intimate searches are going on and at identification parades, video identification and 'confrontations' (a form of identity procedure).

If you are asked to act as someone's appropriate adult then you should if possible make sure that a solicitor is present to help you. The responsibilities being put upon you are considerable, particularly if the allegations against the vulnerable adult are of a serious nature. In most situations the suspect is entitled to legal advice and this is available free under the legal aid scheme (see previous section). The Codes provide that the suspect should always be given the chance of consulting privately with a solicitor in the absence of the appropriate adult if they wish to do so. Now that the right to silence has effectively been abolished it is more important than ever to get good legal advice. As is detailed in Chapter 1, 'Silence Isn't Golden', the court may draw 'such inferences as appear proper' from a failure by the accused person to mention any fact relied on in their defence whilst being questioned under caution or on being charged with the offence. (The appropriate adult will in most cases be present on both those occasions.) Just because the person is a juvenile or has a mental disability does not mean that they have a special right to silence in a police station.[11] However, the question of whether it was reasonable for the person to mention a fact at the time may become an important point for debate and you must be prepared for the eventuality of ending up having to give evidence yourself at the trial.

If you need an 'appropriate adult'

If it is you who is being provided with an appropriate adult and the person called is someone you have never met, consider carefully the extent to which it would be wise to confide in that person. If you talk privately to your lawyer then they are under strict and absolute rules not to tell anyone what you have said and they cannot be forced to give evidence about what you said to them either. The rules about the duties of appropriate adults in this area are not so clear cut. They should not talk to anyone else about what you said to them unless you give them permission to do so, but they do not have the same right that solicitors have not to be called into the witness box to give evidence about what you said.[12]

Notes

Introduction

1. Smith, JC and Brian Hogan, *Criminal Law*, eighth edition, Butterworths, 1996
2. There are also what are called Statutory Instruments which can be made pursuant to a statute.
3. Section 1 (1) of the Protection of Harassment Act 1997
4. In the case of Laskey, Jaggard and Brown v United Kingdom ECHR judgment, 19 February 1997, a group of gay men were sent to prison for having consensual sado-masochistic sex. Until then it was believed that if the adult person assaulted consented to being assaulted the assault would not be a crime.
5. Offences against the Person Act 1861, Section 47
6. Offences against the Person Act 1861, Section 18 (intentional) and Section 20
7. Theft Act 1968, Section 8
8. Theft Act 1968, Section 9
9. Reported in *Guardian*, 7 February 1997 and 8 August 1997.

10. Regina v Thornton (Sara) Court of Appeal, 13 December 1995
11. Notifiable Offences, Home Office Statistical Bulletin, 13 October 1998
12. *The Times*, 14 June 1997
13. *Independent*, 5 November 1997

Chapter 1: First Encounters, the Police and the Crown Prosecution Service

1.   The latest version was released in 1996.
2.   From the CICA Explanatory Booklet: 'If you have not reported the circumstances of the injury to the police, and can offer no reasonable explanation for not doing so, you should assume that any application for compensation will be rejected. Failure to inform the police is unlikely to be excused on the grounds that you feared reprisals, or did not recognise your assailant, or saw no point in reporting it.'
3.   The Crime and Disorder Act 1998, Sections 28–32
4.   Notifiable Offences, the Home Office, 13 October 1998
5.   The Lord Chief Justice, Lord Bingham, has approved the contents of this statement and therefore if its provisions are breached it should be possible to complain.
6.   The Crime and Disorder Act 1998, Section 2. The first such order was made on 23 December 1998 and placed a man recently released from prison after a conviction for rape under night-time curfew after police saw him looking into several houses in the early hours. The order was granted for eight years.
7.   Words said by judges in the case of Rice v Connolly 1966 2AER P649. Also see Notes for Guidance 1B page 5 Code of Practice A, 'All citizens have a duty to help police officers to prevent crime and discover offenders.'
8.   Those who would like to memorise more than is said

here could consider buying the Liberty Guide, *Your Rights*. See Appendix I for more details of this organisation.

9. Defined in PACE as any place to which at the relevant time the public, or any section of the public, has access, on payment or otherwise. Lawyers have had fun arguing about what this actually means.

10. Road Traffic Act 1988, Sections 163 and 165

11. Road Traffic Act 1988, Sections 163 and 168

12. Road Traffic Act 1988, Section 169

13. The Knives Act 1997, which amends the Criminal Justice and Public Order Act 1994

14. Code of Practice A, paragraph 2.4

15. *Guardian*, 27 July 1998, 'Police stop blacks eight times more than whites.'

16. Code of Practice A, paragraph 1.7

17. The term 'arrestable offence' is defined in PACE, Section 24.

18. These relate to factors which the police maintain point to it being difficult to serve a summons on you, such as not knowing your name or address, and to factors suggesting you are vulnerable or that you are likely to cause further trouble. See PACE, Section 25.

19. PACE, Section 28

20. PACE, Section 17

21. Code B, paragraph 5.11

22. Criminal Justice and Public Order Act 1994 (CJPOA), Section 36

23. CJPOA, Section 37

24. You should also be given this caution when you are arrested. Code of Practice C, paragraph 10c.

25. CJPOA, Section 34

26. *ibid*

27. The Crime and Disorder Act 1998, Section 65, now provides that 'young persons' (under 18) are not to be cautioned but will receive a reprimand or a

warning which will result in a referral to the youth offending team. More details are given in Chapter 4.

28. Code of Practice C, paragraph 6.1, PACE, Section 58, and see Chapter 6 for an explanation of how the duty solicitor schemes work.

29. Code of Practice C, paragraph 6.6

30. Code of Practice C, paragraph 2, PACE, Section 36

31. 'Serious arrestable offence' is defined in PACE and includes offences such as murder, rape and offences likely to result in death or serious injury to an individual; serious financial losses or gains; serious damage to state security or public order, or interference with the administration of justice. The criteria are that a senior police officer must certify that they reasonably believe that allowing you to tell someone of your arrest would have various consequences, eg other suspects would be alerted and would get away; evidence, stolen property or ill-gotten gains would disappear, or someone would be harmed. But the solicitor cannot be excluded just because they might advise you not to answer questions nor because someone else, eg a friend, asked them to come, provided you also would like to see them.

32. Code of Practice E, paragraph 3

33. Code of Practice C, paragraph 4.1. The reasons for keeping these items are if the police have grounds to believe that you might use the item to hurt yourself or someone else, to damage property, interfere with evidence or escape, or if the item might be evidence relating to an offence. If you are considered to be or about to become violent or are incapable of understanding what is said to you, the police do not have to tell you why an item has been taken.

34. Code of Practice C, Annexe A, and see above footnote for articles that you would not be allowed to keep.

35. If the situation is urgent and there is a risk of serious

harm to the person detained or to others, then only one person is allowed to do the search. Note that there are special rules for juveniles and adults who need appropriate adults and this is also the case with intimate searches. See Chapter 6.

36. PACE, Section 65
37. In the Misuse of Drugs Act 1971, drugs are put into various categories. Class A are supposed to be the most dangerous, eg heroin.
38. Searches which are not for drugs can be carried out by a same-sex police officer if it is considered not practicable to get the medical person.
39. PACE, Section 65
40. This covers all offences except the most trivial.
41. There are special rules about consenting if the detained person is a juvenile or an adult who needs an appropriate adult, and the same applies in respect of non-intimate samples, fingerprints and photographs. See Chapter 6.
42. There are also provisions for allowing the police in certain circumstances to take such samples after you have been charged or reported for an offence and after conviction.
43. PACE, Section 61
44. See Code D. Photographs of you can be taken if a number of people have been arrested, or if you've been charged or reported for a recordable offence, or after conviction for such if there is no photo on record already, or if authorised by a senior police person if you are suspected of involvement in a criminal offence and there is identification evidence in relation to that offence.
45. Section 64 PACE (fingerprints and samples) Code D photographs. Note that there are exceptions to these provisions in respect of terrorist and immigration matters.

46. See Bail Act 1976. Conditions can be imposed if thought to be necessary to prevent you from absconding, committing another offence or interfering with witnesses etc.

47. Juveniles can be detained for the same reasons and also if detention is considered to be in their interests. The rules about *where* juveniles should be detained are being changed to some extent by the Crime and Disorder Act 1998.

48. PACE, Section 38

49. PACE, Section 46

50. See footnote 46

51. You only don't have to be told the reason if you are incapable of understanding what is said, are violent or likely to become so, or are in urgent need of medical attention.

52. See footnote 31 above

53. PACE, Sections 41 and 42, and note that persons accused of terrorist offences can be held longer.

54. If you have not been charged this person must be an officer of the rank of at least inspector and not involved in the investigation, otherwise it will be the custody sergeant.

55. If the person being detained is juvenile or has a mental disability the appropriate adult can make representations. See Chapter 6.

56. PACE, Section 56 and Code of Practice C, paragraph 5.1

57. A senior police officer must certify that they reasonably believe that allowing you to tell someone of your arrest would have various consequences, eg other suspects would be alerted and would get away, evidence, stolen property or ill-gotten gains would disappear or someone would be harmed.

58. Code of Practice C, paragraph 5.7

59. Code of Practice C, paragraph 5.1

60. Code of Practice C, paragraph 5.6. This is in addition to your right, as set out above, to make a telephone call to a person to tell them you have been arrested. The same rules apply, though, to disallowing these rights as apply to the making of the initial call.
61. Code of Practice C, paragraph 5.4. The custody office can take into account the availability of sufficient manpower to supervise a visit and any possible hindrance to the investigation.
62. Code of Practice C, paragraph 5.5
63. These are lay visitors who should live or work in the borough. They have an independent role and their job is neither to confront nor to collude with the police. They will be concerned to check that the police are treating you as they should.

Chapter 2: In the Criminal Courts

1. See Chapter 5,'Fight Back' section
2. *Yorkshire Post*, 'Talking Dirty', *Guardian*, 30 January 1997
3. Regina v Moringiello, *The Times*, 25 July 1997
4. Appointments to be a judge in the Court of Appeal and House of Lords still do not have to be advertised; cf appointments to the European Court of Human Rights where the job must be advertised. There has been a lot of controversy about the lack of women and ethnic minority judges and stipendiary magistrates. On 1 February 1998 official figures showed that of the 91 stipendiary magistrates, 14 were women and 2 were from ethnic minority groups. Out of a total of 97 High Court Judges, 7 were women and none were from an ethnic minority. Out of 547 circuit judges, 30 were women and ethnic minorities totalled 5. The *Guardian* reported on 1 June 1999 that 'the proportion of women in the judiciary remains 6%, the same as in 1997'.

5. In the *Guardian* of 4 May 1999 it was reported that 4744 judges said they were not masons, 263 said they were and 70 refused to answer. 213 did not reply. 20,300 magistrates said they were not masons, 1208 said they were, 599 refused to answer and 2857 did not reply. It is now being suggested that the names of those who did not reply should be published.

6. At present, offences fall into three categories: those which are so serious that they can only be tried in the crown court, eg murder/manslaughter, rape; those which can be tried in either court depending on the views of the prosecution and the court and subject to the absolute right of the accused to request jury trial regardless of how trivial the matter is perceived to be, eg all types of theft and all types of assault except common assault (refer back to the Introduction); and those which can only be tried in the magistrates' court, eg common assault, many public order and driving related offences. In the case of the middle category, such as theft and assault, the government plans to let the magistrates decide which court the person ought to be tried in, taking into account the gravity of the alleged offence and its complexity. It has been stated that there will be special protection for those who are of good character and that there will be a right of appeal against the magistrates' decision.

7. The Bail Act 1976, Section 4 and Schedule 1, where the exceptions to the right to bail are set out

8. The Bail Act 1976, Schedule 1, part 1, paragraph 9A

9. The Bail Act 1976, as amended by Crime and Disorder Act 1998 Section 56

10. There are some arguments that you can put up to prevent losing the money, eg that you took all reasonable steps to secure the person's attendance. Take advice if you are in this situation as to what to do.

11. The Crime and Disorder Act 1998, Sections 97 and 98, which are not all yet in force, provide for changes in the procedures for remands of juveniles to local authority secure accommodation.

12. The case must be one which is being conducted by or on behalf of the Director of Public Prosecutions and must either be one for which the person could get a prison sentence of over five years or involve vehicle taking or what is called aggravated vehicle taking. The DPP have said, however, that they would only appeal against a bail refusal in cases which are of the greatest concern. 'The nature of the offence and the risk of harm to individual victims are clearly factors which we should take into account' (1994 Annual Report) The Bail (Amendment) Act 1993.

13. Article in *New Law Journal*, 14 November 1997. For details of WAR see Appendix I.

14. *Guardian*, 19 June 1998

15. Telephone the Court Service Headquarters on 0171 210 2110 and ask them to send you a copy if you haven't received one.

16. Home Office leaflet 'Witness in Court' says this facility should be provided.

17. See the above leaflet and the Courts' Charter leaflet, 'Witnesses in the Crown Court'.

18. July 1996. A Home Office report released in June 1998 also recommended that a number of provisions be made to assist witnesses, including better protection against intimidation. The Victim's Charter also advises victims to contact the police if they fear being attacked or harassed as a result of a court case.

19. The Crown Court Charter says also that they aim to keep you waiting no more than two hours, but if you do have to wait longer then someone will 'tell you why and indicate how long the wait may be'.

20. The Criminal Justice Act 1988, Section 32A, as

amended. This Act also provides that in certain circumstances videos of the child giving a statement can be used leaving the child to have to deal only with live cross examination. There are calls for proposed legislation presently proceeding through Parliament to provide more protection for children from hostile cross-examination.

21. If when you get to the court and before you give your evidence you would like to read through your statement again you can ask the CPS to let you have a copy.

22. The government wishes to make it illegal for a defendant accused of rape to cross-examine the victim personally. At the time of writing proposed legislation was proceeding through Parliament.

23. 'Witness in Court' leaflet

24. The Sexual Offences (Amendment) Act 1976, Sections 2 and 7 (2). There has been considerable controversy about the way judges have exercised their discretion in this area and it is possible that reforms will take place.

25. 'Witness in Court' leaflet. 'National Standards of Witness Care', Archbold, *Criminal Pleadings, Evidence and...*, Sweet & Maxwell, 1999, section 8–69

26. The Sexual Offences (Amendment) Act 1976, Section 4; The Sexual Offences (Amendment) Act 1992, Sections 1–4

27. Children and Young Persons Act 1933, Section 39

28. Juveniles are usually tried in the youth court. The government is aiming to reduce the time taken from arrest of young offenders to the start of the trial to 28 days.

29. See Chapter 6 for advice about the duty solicitor scheme and how to find a suitable lawyer.

30. Magistrates' Courts (Advance Information) Rules 1985. You don't have the right to any advance

information or statements if the offence is one which can only be tried in the magistrates' court, but it is still worth hassling the Crown Prosecution Service to give you details of the case against you. If they refuse, you arguably have a good basis upon which to complain.

31. See footnote 6 for details of plans to curtail the right to ask for jury trial.

32. See section on bail for your rights to be released on bail pending your trial. See Chapter 3 on prisons for your rights on remand if you are not granted bail.

33. The Crime and Disorder Act 1998, Section 51. If you are also charged with other related offences which can be tried in the crown court, if you agree then you can be sent straight up for those at the same time.

34. The Criminal Procedure and Investigations Act 1996, Section 11

35. *ibid*., Section 3. You will be served a notice setting all this out.

36. The Criminal Justice and Public Order Act 1994, Section 35

37. See witness section above

38. The Criminal Justice and Public Order Act 1994, Section 48

39. See Chapter 4, 'Side Effects', for what can happen if a fine is not paid back as ordered.

40. If legal aid has been previously refused because the matter was considered not to be serious enough then you can now try again and you will no doubt be successful unless you are too 'rich'.

41. Guidance to the Justices Clerks Society in 1998 stated that if this happens the defendant who has been on bail should be allowed to stay on bail unless there were substantial grounds to believe they might abscond or commit further offences.

42. Victim's Charter, Archbold, *Criminal Pleadings*,

Evidence and ..., Sweet & Maxwell, 1999, Section 5–22
43. Victim's Charter and The Criminal Justice Act 1988, Section 36

Chapter 3: In Prison

1. *Guardian* 30 June 1988
2. See Chapter 4, 'Side Effects'
3. *Guardian* editorial, 22 November 1998
4. For young offenders the relevant rules are the Young Offender Institution Rules 1988 as amended in 1999. There are plans to draw up a new set later in 1999.
5. The *Prisoners' Information Handbook* is presently being updated, but in any event Prison Rule 10 (1) says that every prisoner shall be provided, as soon as possible after their reception into prison, and in any case within 24 hours, with information in writing about those provisions of the Prison Rules and other matters 'which it is necessary that he should know, including earnings and privileges and the proper means of making requests and complaints'.
6. 'Ms Forsyth, a financial adviser who had never been in prison before, was forced to serve her sentence inside a high security prison because there are only three open prisons for women compared with 15 for men.' *Law Society Gazette*, 1 October 1997, Mr Krivinskas, solicitor who represented Elizabeth Forsyth of Polly Peck fame.
7. Prison Rule 12. Roisin McAliskey, for instance, was kept for a while in Belmarsh prison in London.
8. See the case of Regina v Accrington Youth Court and others ex. p. Flood, *New Law Journal*, 17 October 1997. The Crime and Disorder Act 1998, parts of which are not yet in force, contains provisions which will alter the way in which all ages of young

offenders are dealt with when committed to custody. There isn't space here to detail all the provisions.

9. Prison Rule 7 (2) (b)
10. Prison Rule 20 (5)
11. Prison Rule 35 (1). Some women have been put off exercising their rights to lots of visits on remand because they have been strip-searched after each one. If this happens take advice about whether to complain.
12. Prison Rule 7(3)
13. See Prison Rule 41. Also Security Manual, Paragraph 17, point 22, says that intimate searches of prisoners are not allowed unless the prisoner consents or a court authorises one on medical grounds. Take advice at once if you hear that any such court application is to be made.
14. Prison Rule 43
15. *New Law Journal*, 20 February 1998, 'A bold vision of decency'
16. Disciplinary offences are dealt with later on in this chapter. Note that unconvicted prisoners come within this system as well.
17. Prison Rule 8 (4)
18. Prison Rule 28
19. Prison Rule 31
20. Prison Rule 24 (1) (2)
21. Prison Rule 25
22. Prison Rules 29 and 30
23. Prison Rule 32. If the offender is aged under 17 arrangements must be made for their participation in education or training courses for at least 15 hours a week within the normal working week.
24. Prison Rule 33
25. See Prison Rule 20. All prisons have now been circulated with a report which advises that midwifery care for pregnant prisoners should be

provided by the local NHS community midwifery services. New health care standards for pregnant women and babies are expected in 1999.

26. Prison Rule 21
27. Prison Rules 35 and 34
28. See Prison Rule 39. The grounds are: illicit enclosures, danger to prison security or safety of others, otherwise of a criminal nature. In a court case it has also been decided that if your cell is searched the authorities can inspect correspondence to ensure it is bona fide legal correspondence.
29. Prison Rule 35. Note that 'closed visits', ie those where physical contact between prisoner and visitor is prevented, can be imposed if the Secretary of State requires it (Prison Rule 34 (2)).
30. Prison Rule 38
31. Rule 35. Recently, a case was heard in the House of Lords where two journalists who wanted to visit prisoners were required first to sign an undertaking that any material obtained would not be used for professional purposes, especially for publication by the journalists or anyone else. The prisoners challenged the imposition of this condition. Regina v Secretary of State for Home Department ex parte Simms, O'Brien, Main. 8 July 1999, the House of Lords held an indiscriminate ban on journalists' visits was unlawful.
32. Prison Rule 71 (1)
33. Prison Rule 73. 'Guidance to Governors' suggests that family members will normally be banned for three months and then for the next three months only closed visits (see footnote 29) will be allowed.
34. The sorts of organisations presently approved are, eg, the Samaritans, the Citizens Advice Bureaux, the Prisoners Advice Service.
35. Prison Rule 9

36. Young offenders have the same right to have their babies with them but may have to care for them in a unit where there are adult offenders.
37. Prison Rule 50
38. Prison Rules 53 and 54
39. Prison Rule 55. Rule 57 says that in the case of most young offenders under 21 privileges are only to be stopped for up to 21 days and cellular confinement can only be up to 7 days. Earnings stoppages are to be for a shorter period also.
40. Prison Rule 47
41. Prison Rule 45. The criteria are that it is desirable for the maintenance of good order or discipline or in your own interests.
42. Prison Rule 46. The criteria are the same as in note 41, but also to ensure the safety of others in the prison. If such a direction is made the provisions of Rule 45 do not apply.
43. Prison Rule 48. Special or strip cells have only a mattress in them or possibly cardboard furniture.
44. Prison Rule 49. The sort of restraints used must be authorised by the Secretary of State. Body belts, ie leather belts with handcuffs attached to restrict movement, have been used.
45. The Crime and Disorder Act 1998, Section 58
46. The Criminal Justice Act 1991, Schedule 5
47. Daniels v Griffiths (*Law Society Gazette*, 17 December 1997; Court of Appeal 27 November 1997)
48. Prison Rule 5

Chapter 4: Side Effects

1. Regina v Hereford Magistrates' Court ex. MacRae, *Law Society Gazette*, 15 December 1998
2. A means enquiry must be held before you can be sent to prison for not paying a fine. This too was said in the above case.

3. This is all in the Magistrates' Courts Act 1980. If you are sent to prison because you have not paid a fine then to some extent you are entitled to be treated differently to sentenced prisoners.

4. Schedule 1B IS (General) Regulations, 1987

5. Housing Benefit (General) Regulations 1987, as amended

6. The Criminal Justice Act 1988, Section 71(1A)

7. The Children and Young Persons Act 1933, Section 55

8. The Children Act 1989

9. The Crime and Disorder Act 1998, Sections 11 and 12

10. The Crime and Disorder Act 1998, Sections 14 and 15

11. The Crime and Disorder Act 1998, Sections 65 and 66. This new system will replace the previous system whereby a caution had to be considered.

12. The Crime and Disorder Act, Sections 8 and 9

13. The Contempt of Court Act 1981

14. The Children and Young Persons Act 1933, unless the court later directs otherwise

15. Brown (Gordon) v DPP, 12 March 1998; *Law Society Gazette*, 29 April 1998

16. In some cases young offenders can treat a conviction as spent in half the time an adult has to wait for.

17. Children (Protection from Offenders) (Miscellaneous Amendments) Regulations 1997 SI 1997/2308. These rules are giving rise to concern in some cases and if it is felt that despite these rules it would be in the child's best interests to remain in a placement even if one of the carers has a past relevant conviction then sometimes other procedures can be used to effect this. Re RJ (fostering, wardship) 1999 FL 90).

18. In Chapter 2 we mentioned sex offender orders

which can be made to control the behaviour of a sex offender after their release from prison. Section 58 of the Crime and Disorder Act 1998 has also introduced extended licences for offenders convicted of sexual or violent offences.

Chapter 5: Fight Back

1. The Police and Criminal Evidence Act 1984
2. These payments are presently 'ex gratia' (voluntary) but the Access to Justice Bill presently going through Parliament may include a provision for a statutory right to claim compensation for wrongful behaviour by the courts.
3. On 23 April 1999, *The Times* reported 2109 complaints were made against judges between August 1998 and June 1999. Of these, 183 where the complaint involved personal conduct were investigated, and further action taken. Lord Irvine has censured 5 judges over their personal conduct in court after complaints from lawyers and members of the public.
4. Due to recent reorganisation of the CPS, a new complaints procedure may soon be issued.
5. The system of dealing with complaints about solicitors may be reformed in the future to introduce an element of independence from the Law Society. Note that you may also have the right to sue the solicitor in the civil courts (see next section), which may be important, as the OSS's power to award compensation is limited and is not intended to compensate for a serious episode of negligence. If a solicitor has actually stolen money from you then the Solicitors' Compensation Fund will pay the money back even if the solicitor has disappeared with it.
6. It is difficult to sue barristers because advocates can still claim 'immunity from suit' in respect of their

advocacy. This rule applies to solicitor advocates too.

7. Prison Rule 11
8. '£25,000 for family of shackled prisoner', *The Times*, 16 June 1998, referring to a case where a man who was dying of cancer was shackled to his bed for 11 days, the shackles only being removed 3 hours before he died.
9. For instance, after Lynn Siddons was murdered the family brought a civil case against a man who had never been prosecuted for the murder. Their civil action was successful and thereafter the man was prosecuted and found guilty.
10. Legislation presently going through Parliament may change this to a 60–80 per cent chance of winning, and the costs-benefit ratio may be that the damages must be at least three times the expected costs. There is also a possibility that legal aid will be abolished for all cases where damages are being claimed which will mean that everyone will have to use the no-win-no-fee system or represent themselves.
11. Legal aid is likely to be limited on a step-by-step basis. As the case progresses your lawyers will have to ask permission from the Legal Aid Board to take each new step. They will also have to report regularly to the Board to say whether the case is still worth pursuing.
12. Commissioner of Police for the Metropolis v Thompson, Hsu v Commissioner of Police for the Metropolis Court of Appeal, 19 February 1997. The figures given could now be increased appropriately to take inflation into account.
13. Hill v Chief Constable of West Yorkshire 1989, AC 53, HL
14. Osman v UK, 28 October 1998; 87/1997/871/1083
15. Haywood v Somerfield Stores Ltd (T/A Food Giant.)

Current Law, September Digest 169, 9 July 1997 Nuneaton CC

16. In a test case reported in the *Guardian* on 20 June 1998, the Court of Appeal ruled that inmates who had their sentences wrongly calculated were entitled to compensation. In a case where a male prisoner was shackled to his bed for 11 days whilst dying of cancer, his family were offered £25,000 compensation by the Prison Service, *The Times*, 18 June 1998.

17. *Solicitors Journal*, 12 September 1997

18. *Guardian*, 5 November 1997

19. The case was brought by Carolyn Parrington. *Guardian*, 20 February 1999.

20. The Powers of Criminal Courts Act 1973, Section 35 (1)

21. The Crime and Disorder Act 1988 Sections 67 and 68. For instance, an offender who snatched a 68-year-old's handbag offered to do supervised voluntary work in a local retirement home.

22. In a case reported in *Current Law*, February Digest 1998, it was held that a woman who was a victim of regular obscene and sexually threatening telephone calls which continued over two years could claim compensation under the scheme for the mental trauma she suffered as a result.

23. In order to obtain a conviction for a criminal offence the court must be sure beyond all reasonable doubt that the offender is guilty of the offence. In the civil court the court needs only to find that the allegations are proved on the balance of probabilities. The CICA has adopted the latter, less stringent, test.

24. There must have been good reason for the delay and it must be in the interests of justice for the late claim to be allowed.

25. Tay House, 300 Bath Street, Glasgow G2 4JR

26. The introduction of this system was highly contro-

versial and the use of it to offer Josie Russell only £18,500 for the loss of her mother and sister has been criticised. *Guardian*, 2 April 1998. Later an extra £60,000 was offered. *Guardian*, 30 July 1998. It is possible that the fixed tariffs will be reviewed.

27. See Appendix I for further details of this organisation.

28. See next section for more discussion about judicial review. In the case of Regina v Criminal Injuries Compensation Board, ex. p. K and ors. 30 July 1998, the High Court allowed an application challenging a decision by the CICB reducing an award to children following their mother's death. This is a difficult area and one where advice definitely needs to be taken.

29. This may well be the case in circumstances as in footnote 28, above, where a claim is being made on behalf of children who have lost a parent due to a crime being committed.

30. The Criminal Justice Act 1988, Section 133 as amended. It was announced in May 1999 that compensation is also to be paid to the surviving relatives of Derek Bentley (hanged at the age of 19 for murder and pardoned after his conviction was quashed in July 1998).

31. The Coroners Act 1988, Section 8

32. Coroners Rules 1984, Rule 20. The people who may ask questions include parents, spouse, and children and persons whom the coroner considers to be 'properly interested'. 'The word "interested" should not be given a narrow technical meaning, nor is it confined to a proprietary right or a financial interest in the deceased's estate, but can cover a variety of concerns.' *Levine on Coroners Courts*, Sweet and Maxwell, 1999.

33. Coroners Rules 1984, Rule 43. 'A coroner who believes that action should be taken to prevent the

recurrence of fatalities similar to that in respect of which the inquest is being held may announce at the inquest that he is reporting the matter in writing to the person or authority who may have power to take such action and he may report the matter accordingly.'

34. Following the Stephen Lawrence inquiry the government have said they will make legal aid for inquests available in 'exceptional cases' only. The inquiry recommended it be available in all 'appropriate cases'.

35. This followed one of the recommendations of the Stephen Lawrence inquiry and the Home Secretary has said that disclosure of documentary material to interested parties before the inquest will now become usual practice. A Code of Practice has been issued and the disclosure should only be refused if there is a good reason, such as prejudice to an on-going criminal investigation.

36. Shiji Lapite died in December 1994 of asphyxia from compression of the neck consistent with the application of a neck hold by a Stoke Newington police officer. The inquest jury returned a unanimous verdict that he had been unlawfully killed. Richard O'Brien was a 37-year-old Irishman. On 4 April 1994 he died within 10 minutes of his arrest for allegedly being drunk and disorderly. On 10 November 1995 the inquest jury decided he had been unlawfully killed.

37. Under the Police Act 1996, Section 49.

38. You may need to refer back to Chapter 1, 'Reporting a crime and obtaining protection', to understand this one.

39. See footnotes 34 and 35 above and also the implementation of a recent change to the Police Complaints system referred to earlier in this chapter

which followed a recommendation of the inquiry.

40. *Guardian*, 22 April 1999

41. Section 26 of the Criminal Appeals Act 1995 amending S142 Magistrates' Courts Act 1980

42. If you are serving a prison sentence you may be warned that if you go on with the appeal you may end up being kept in for longer. Take advice if this happens.

43. The Criminal Appeals Act 1995, Section 2

44. The Criminal Justice Act 1988, Section 36

45. CCRC, Alpha Tower, Suffolk Street, Queensway, Birmingham B1 1TT; tel. 0121 633 1800

46. *Guardian*, 31 January 1998

Chapter 6: Advice and Representation

1. For example, there are personal injury panels and a solicitor who is not on a special panel is not allowed to represent a child who is the subject of care proceedings.

2. In some situations a form of legal aid called ABWOR (Assistance By Way Of Representation) may be available for fine defaulters but in most cases they will be expected to go to the duty solicitor.

3. In the future your rights to put the case off to see your chosen solicitor may be restricted.

4. Legal Aid Act 1988, Section 22 (2)

5. Don't forget that if you are representing yourself and there is a risk of a prison sentence you must be warned of the peril you are in so that you can think about applying for legal aid.

6. Published by Civil Liberties Trust, 21 Tabard Street, London SE1, 1995, £4.99

7. This name derives from the case which first established this right.

8. Thanks to Lisa Barcan at the Tate Library, Brixton

9. The organisation Mencap have produced a very

helpful leaflet called 'How To Be an "Appropriate Adult": some facts'. Contact Mencap National Centre, 123 Golden Lane, London EC1Y 0RT.

10. The Crime and Disorder Act 1998 is bringing in, in respect of juveniles, a duty upon local authorities to provide suitable people to act as 'appropriate adults'.

11. In the 'Not Guilty' section I detail the extent to which special consideration can be given at the trial to vulnerable defendants.

12. There are plans to change this and put appropriate adults in the same position as solicitors.

Appendix I
Advice Agencies, Campaigning Groups and Professional Bodies

Age Concern England, Astral House, 1268 London Road, London SW16 4ER, 0800 009 966

Alzheimer's Disease Society, Gordon House, 10 Greencoat Place, London SW1P 1PH, helpline: 0845 300 0336

Bar Council, 3 Bedford Row, London WC1, enquiries: 0171 242 0082

Children's Legal Centre, University of Essex, Wivenhoe Park, Colchester, Essex CO4 3SQ, advice line: 01206 873 820

ChildLine, 0800 1111

Citizens Advice Bureaux (CAB). The central body for the CAB movement is NACAB , Myddleton House, 115 Pentonville Road, London N1 9LZ, 0171 833 2181. Wherever you live there should be one of these reasonably near to you. They offer advice about a very wide range of problems. They use volunteers a lot but all of them are trained and some of them are qualified lawyers who offer their services free at evening advice sessions. If you wish to claim compensation from the CICA then they should be able to give you advice about how to go about it. If you want to find a solicitor who can help with your particular problem they should have details of a suitable one. They also give advice about such matters as entitlement to benefits and housing problems. The CAB do outreach work in prisons. They cannot advise about the matter that led to you being in prison but they can advise about arrival procedures, how to complain, prison visits, punishment and health issues. Some CAB run advice desks at magistrates' courts and they could help you there, particularly if you have a problem, for example about how to pay a fine. Also they can advise you about your children and give you advice about leaving prison.

Inquest, Ground Floor, Alexandra National House, 330 Seven Sisters Road, London N4 2PJ, 0181 802 7430. Inquest campaigns against police and prison related deaths and for changes in the coroner's court system. The organisation monitors deaths in custody throughout Britain, in police custody and at the hands of the police, in prison and in immigration detention centres. Inquest provides a free legal and advice service to the bereaved on inquest procedure and their basic rights in the coroner's court. If someone close to you has died as a result of a brush with the criminal justice system or if there is to be an inquest into the death of someone close to you and you want advice, this is the organisation to contact.

Joint Council for the Welfare of Immigrants, 115 Old Street, London EC1V 9RT, advice line: 0171 251 8706

Justice, 59 Carter Lane, London EC4V 5AQ, 0171 329 5100. Justice is an independent legal human-rights organisation which aims to improve British justice. It was founded to champion law reform and human rights. The organisation was instrumental in the establishment of the Criminal Cases Review Commission (see previous section). Justice campaigns actively in the areas of human rights and miscarriages of justice.

Justice for Women, 55 Rathcoole Gardens, London N8 9NE, 0181 374 2948. There are also offices in Manchester, Norwich and Bradford. Justice for Women aims to monitor and raise awareness of the response of the criminal justice system to male violence and to publicise and challenge the outcome of specific court cases where women have been unfairly treated in respect of male violence. The Justice for Women Campaign also aims to change the law so that it recognises and takes seriously women's experience of male violence.

Law centres. The centralised body for the law centres movement is the Law Centres Federation, Duchess House, 18–19 Warren Street, London W1P 5DP, 0171 387 8570. In some areas of the country there are local law centres. These provide a free and independent professional legal service to people who live and work in their catchment area. They might be able to help you claim compensation from the CICA and if you want to find an appropriate lawyer they should be able to point you in the right direction. Sometimes they take on a case themselves but the sort of work they are allowed and able to take on is limited. They often advise on welfare rights and housing.

Law Society, 113 Chancery Lane, London WC2A 1PL, 0171 242 1222

Liberty (National Council for Civil Liberties), 21 Tabard Street, London SE1 4LA, 0171 403 3888. An independent, non-government organisation working to defend and extend the civil and political rights of people in Britain. Liberty mounts campaigns, takes on test cases and gives advice and information. Areas covered which are particularly relevant to this book are police powers, miscarriages of justice and the right to a fair trial.

London Rape Crisis Centre, 0171 916 5466. For women or girls who have been sexually assaulted. There are many other local rape crisis centres.

Mencap (Royal Society for Mentally Handicapped Children and Adults), 123 Golden Lane, London EC1Y ORT, 0171 454 0454

Mind (National Association of Mental Health), Granta House, 15–19 Broadway, London E15 4BQ, London information: 0181 522 1728; outside London: 0345 660 163

National Association for the Care and Resettlement of Offenders. The centralised body is Nacro Services, 169, Clapham Road, London SW9 OPU, 0171 582 6500. NACRO may be able to help you with advice about matters such as your housing and employment after release. NACRO runs some hostel accommodation and training centres. They have a Women Prisoners Resource Centre which can offer advice and information to women prisoners: London WPRC (for Holloway, Bullwood Hall, Cookham Wood, East Sutton Park), Office 1A, 383 Canalside House, London W10 5AA, 0181 968 3121; North East WPRC, Back on Track, Outwood Hall, Victoria Street, Outwood, Wakefield WF1 2NN, 01924 820 970.

NSPCC, 42 Curtain Road, London EC2A 3NH, helpline: 0800 800 500

Prisoners Advice Service, Unit 305, Hatton Square, 16/16A Baldwins Gardens, London EC1N 7RJ, 0171 405 8090. This organisation provides advice and information to prisoners in England and Wales regarding their rights, particularly concerning the application of the Prison Rules and the conditions of their imprisonment. PAS will help with prisoners' complaints and also with applications for parole. PAS also campaigns about penal issues.

Refugee Legal Centre, Sussex House, 39–45 Bermondsey Street, London SE1 3XF, advice: 0171 378 6242

Rights of Women, 52–54 Featherstone Street, London EC1Y 8RT, advice: 0171 251 6577

Shelter (National Campaign for Homeless People), Shelterline: 0808 800 4444

Victim Support. The Victim Support National Office is at Cranmer House, 39 Brixton Road, London SW9 6DZ, 0171 735 9166. Victim Support has branches all over the country and they state that they 'provide emotional support, practical help and information to people who have suffered crimes ranging from burglary to the murder of a relative'. This would include helping you apply for compensation from the CICA. They also run a witness service in all the crown court centres. Victim Support say that trained volunteers 'offer emotional support and information to victims and witnesses of crime before, during and after hearings in the crown court'. If you have to go to a crown court to give evidence a Victim Support person may come up to you as you come into the door. The person can show you around an empty court room explaining where everyone sits and the person will stick with you and offer you support until you are free or want to go. The person can help smuggle you out of a back door, for instance, if this is necessary. Long term support is also offered to some victims and Victim Support have given special consideration to female victims of rape and sexual assault. There is also a Victim Support telephone line: 0845 30 30 900.

Voice UK, P.O. Box 238, Derby DE1 9JN, 01332 519 872 is a support and information group for people with learning disabilities who have been abused, their families and carers. They also campaign for changes in the law and practice in this area. They provide a telephone support line, parents' meetings, tele-conferences and a national network of parent contact points.

Women Against Rape, Crossroads Women's Centre, 230a Kentish Town Road, London NW5 2AB, 0171 482 2496. They give support, counselling, legal advice and information to women and girls who have been raped or sexually assaulted. They also campaign on a number of relevant issues, eg for fair and respectful treatment from the police and courts of survivors of rape. If a woman who does not live in London rings for help they will try and put her in touch with local services. For instance, there might be a Rape Crisis Centre in your area. Based at the same address and telephone number is also the organisation Legal Action for Women, which is a grassroots, anti-sexist, anti-racist legal service for all women.

Women's Aid Federation, England, P.O. Box 391, Bristol BS99 7WS, advice: 0345 023 468

Women in Prison, 22 Highbury Grove, London N5 2EA, 0171 226 5879. This organisation sends workers into some prisons, at present Holloway, Bullwood Hall, Highpoint, East Sutton Park and Eastwood, and has a freephone line to them for prisoners to use. They will offer advice to women prisoners, particularly on issues like housing, eg retaining your tenancy while in prison, the Prison Rules, eg your right to visits, and will help you if, for example, you are not happy with your solicitor and want to change them. If you are in Holloway you could also ask to see the Legal Aid and Bail Unit. They will help you contact sureties or your solicitor and they will offer advice about bail hostels and help you fill out appeal forms.

Appendix II
Official Bodies

Criminal Cases Review Commission, Alpha Tower, Suffolk Street, Queensway, Birmingham B1 1TT, 0121 633 1800. An independent body responsible for investigating suspected miscarriages of criminal justice in England, Wales and Northern Ireland.

Criminal Injuries Compensation Authority, Tay House, 300 Bath Street, Glasgow G2 4JR, 0141 331 2726. This organisation is funded by the government to award compensation to victims of crimes of violence. It operates the Criminal Injuries Compensation Scheme established under the Criminal Injuries Compensation Act 1995.

Crown Prosecution Service Headquarters, 50 Ludgate Hill, London EC4M 7EX, enquiries: 0171 334 8505. The CPS was set up in 1986 to prosecute criminal cases resulting from police investigations in England and Wales. The CPS makes the decision as to whether to continue with a case which the police have investigated; if they do go on with it they are the ones who bring it to court.

Customer Service Unit, The Court Service, Southside, 105 Victoria Street, London SW1E 6QT, 0171 210 2269. The CSU will provide further information about the courts service and can investigate complaints which have not been resolved with the Court concerned.

Legal Services Ombudsman, Oxford Court, 22 Oxford Street, Manchester M2 3WQ, 0161 236 9532. Appointed by the Lord Chancellor to oversee the handling of complaints about solicitors, barristers and licensed conveyancers by their respective professional bodies.

Police Complaints Authority, 10 Great George Street, London SW1P 3AE, 0171 273 6450. This authority was set up under the Police and Criminal Evidence Act 1984 with three basic functions: to supervise the most serious complaints against police officers, to review the outcome of every investigation whether supervised or not, and to supervise non-complaint matters which raise grave or exceptional issues such as shooting incidents, deaths in police custody and serious corruption.

Appendix III
Reading List

Child Poverty Action Group, *The Welfare Benefits Handbook*. A 2-volume set priced £20 (£5 to benefits claimants) is available from 0171 837 7979.

Devlin, Angela, *Invisible Women: What's Wrong with Women's Prisons?*, Waterside Press, 1998

Disability Alliance, *Disability Rights Handbook*, the Disability Alliance, Universal House, 88–94 Wentworth Street, London E1 7SA, 0171 247 8776. A guide to benefits and services for all disabled people, their families, carers and advisers.

Leech, Mark, *The Prisons Handbook*, Waterside Press, to be published annually in November

Lees, Sue, *Carnal Knowledge: Rape on Trial*, Penguin, 1997

London Rape Crisis Centre, *Sexual Violence: The Reality*

for Women, The Women's Press, 3rd edition, 1999

Randle, Michael, *How to Defend Yourself in Court*, Civil Liberties Trust, 1995

Your Rights: The Liberty Guide, NCCL with Pluto Press, 1998. Advice about all aspects of civil liberties.

Index